The CEO's Playbook for Scale

The Only Guide You Need to Start, Grow, Scale, and Exit Your Business Successfully

By Eric T. Whitmoyer

Founder & CEO My Biz Coaches

Host of The Biz Coach Show

Published by Biz Coach Publishing

The CEO's Playbook for Scale

The Only Guide You Need to Start, Grow, Scale, and Exit Your Business Successfully

Disclaimer

This publication is designed to provide accurate and authoritative information regarding business strategy, leadership, financial performance, operational systems, and scaling enterprises. It is sold with the understanding that the author and publisher are not engaged in rendering legal, accounting, financial, tax, or other professional services.

The strategies, frameworks, competencies, and models described; including the **7 Core Competencies** and **8 Phases of Scale**; are based on the author's professional experience and research. Results may vary depending on execution, industry conditions, economic factors, and leadership decisions.

Readers are encouraged to seek appropriate professional advice tailored to their specific situation before implementing any business strategy described in this book.

Trademark Notice

"My Biz Coaches," "The CEO's Playbook for Scale," "The 7 Core Competencies," "The 8 Phases of Scale," "The Biz Coach Show," "My Biz Navigator", and related marks are trademarks of My Biz Coaches, LLC.

All other trademarks referenced herein are the property of their respective owners.

ISBN

ISBN-13: 978-1-972657-01-0 - Print
ISBN-13: 978-1-972657-00-3 - Digital

Publisher Information

Published by:
Biz Coach Publishing
Chandler, AZ
United States of America
BizCoachPublishing.com
Info@BizCoachPublishing.com

For bulk orders, speaking engagements, coaching inquiries, or partnership opportunities:
Info@MyBizcoaches.co

Table Of Contents:

Acknowledgements 7

Introduction 9

Section I – The Failure Epidemic

1. Welcome to Entrepreneurship 12

2. Understanding Small Business Failure 29

3. Market Research and Demand: Is There a Need? 36

4. Crafting a Solid Business Plan 41

5. Financing and Cash-Flow Management 47

6. Pricing Strategies and Profitability 54

7. Marketing: Reaching and Engaging Customers 58

8. Management and Leadership Skills 63

9. Building and Nurturing a Winning Team 68

10. Competition and Differentiation 72

11. Location and Digital Presence 76

12. Adaptation to Market Changes 80

13. Scaling and Sustainable Growth 84

14. Legal, Regulatory, and Risk Management 88

15. External Factors and Crisis Preparedness 92

16. Exiting the Business: Succession and Exit Planning 96

Section II – The Solution Framework

17. The 7 Core Competencies: Forged in the Field, Proven in the Fire 102

18. The Bedrock of the 7 Core Competencies: Leadership & Vision – The Growth Ceiling 118

19. Financial Acumen: The Control System 127

20. Sales & Marketing: The Growth Engine 139

21. Operational Excellence: The Duplication Machine 149

22. People Management: The Multiplier Effect 156

23. Customer Focus: The Profit Stabilizer 169

24. The 7th Core Competency: Technology & Innovation Resilience & Relevance 182

Section III – The 8 Phases of Scale

25. The 8 Phases of Scale: From Creator to Enterprise 190

26. Integrating the 7 Core Competencies into The 8 Phases of Scale 201

Section IV – Exit, Transferability & Legacy

27. From Startup to Exit: Begin with the End in Mind 215

Section V – Summing It All Up

28. The Entrepreneur's Dream: Discipline, Scale, and the Path Forward 238

BONUS

Introduction of the 7 Core Competencies Assessment and the My Biz Navigator™ App. 252

References 260

About The Author 262

Special Offers 264

Acknowledgements

I always have to give thanks to anyone and everyone who played a role in bringing a book to life. I couldn't possibly remember everyone, however, to those who provided insights and conversations that made an impact in breathing life into this book, while others provided unbelievable ongoing support – Thank you All!

To those who played a slightly bigger role, I have included a short list here:

Lloyd Dill	Laura Boone	Katrena Pitts
Lacy Ingraham	Rudy Swigart	Katrena Drake
Walt Lipsky	Chris Flowers	Joe Smith
Carlos Cruz	Xavier Marin	Ron Mora
Candice Turalba	Adrianna Marin	David Macon
Carly Whiteside	Victoria Dorsano	Rachel Whitenhafer

My ENO Networking Group – The Caffeinated Mastermind Group

And to all our clients over the last 6 years – MASSIVE THANK YOU, for the role you played!

To my mentors who have guided me throughout my journey, whether you are actively involved in my projects or because your conversations and coaching continue to stay with me, you all played a role in this. Darren Yager, Todd Heiner, Jeff Heuple, Rob

Bean, Denny Meyer, Jack Canfield, and of course my father, John Whitmoyer.

Additional thanks to our team at My Biz Coaches, you are outstanding and we are building something even more amazing and I am extremely excited for the future!

To my little brother and partner at Partner Pro Marketing Solutions, Ian Whitmoyer, thank you for seeing the vision and being willing to jump in and ride this crazy train of entrepreneurship!

Extra Special thanks to my Executive Assistant, Christine Carrera. Your commitment and passion is greatly appreciated and your loyalty, drive and work ethic has been amazing this past year. I don't believe I can share enough how much your efforts have improved My Biz Coaches and all of our projects! Without you NONE of this would have come together – THANK YOU!

And, as always, none of what I do would be worth it without the love and support from my family! My parents, my brothers and sisters, and most importantly my kids, Jasmine and Jonathan, my grandchildren; Jonathan, Jaxon, Vivian, Charlotte, and Carter.

And of course, my beautiful wife Lidia. Without her support none of this would be possible or worth it. If I can't share my accomplishments with you, it's like it never happened. Thank you for everything – I Love You!

Introduction

Every year, hundreds of thousands of new businesses are started, and as of the writing of this book there are approximately 34.5 million businesses in the United States alone. Entrepreneurs are fueled by optimism and determination, yet statistics paint a sobering picture. According to the U.S. Bureau of Labor Statistics, nearly one in four private-sector businesses fail in their first year, nearly half are gone within five years, and almost three-fourths do not survive a decade[1]. A 2024 review of businesses that opened in 2002 shows that 23.8 % failed within the first year, 49.9 % failed within five years and 72.8 % closed within ten years[2]. These figures reveal a simple truth: failure is more common than success.

Why do so many ventures close their doors? Researchers at Service Corps of Retired Executives (SCORE) and others have shown that cash-flow problems are the leading killer of small businesses, contributing to the demise of more than 80% of failed firms[3]. Yet running out of money is only one symptom of deeper issues. Studies and analyses from the U.S. Chamber of Commerce, Investopedia, Georgia's Small Business Development Center and numerous financial institutions identify recurring themes: Insufficient market demand, poor planning, lack of financing, ineffective marketing, weak management, bad pricing and inability to adapt to change[4][5][6][7]. Understanding these root causes provides entrepreneurs with a roadmap for avoiding common pitfalls.

Equally important is grasping the scale of the challenge. When you know that almost half of startups will not survive five years and almost three-fourths will fold within ten years[8], you appreciate how high the stakes are. Failures are not always due to incompetence; often they stem from underestimating how much capital is required to weather slow periods, misjudging the market's appetite or growing too quickly without proper systems[7]. Economic conditions, supply-chain disruptions, inflation and regulatory changes also play a role. In 2024 inflation remained stubbornly well above 3 %, which squeezed margins for many new businesses[9].

This book is a comprehensive guide for entrepreneurs, business owners and anyone who wishes to understand why companies stumble and how to build an enterprise that endures. Each chapter, in this first section, tackles one of the major reasons behind business failure, backed by research, statistics and real-world examples. Rather than providing generic advice, the book digs into the underlying drivers of success and failure; from market analysis and planning to leadership, cash-flow management and crisis preparedness. It also offers actionable strategies for turning challenges into opportunities and emphasizes the importance of adaptability and continuous learning.

The aim is not to discourage entrepreneurship but to empower readers. By learning from others' mistakes, business owners can avoid repeating them. Recognizing that 35% of startups fail because there is no market need for their product or service[10] or that nearly 20% collapse due to team problems[11] allows founders to focus on customer research and team building early on. By understanding that poor planning underlies most failures and that a solid business plan is indispensable[12], entrepreneurs can invest time and resources into creating a roadmap that anticipates challenges and outlines solutions.

In the pages that follow, you will find a structured exploration of the factors that cause businesses to fail, followed by practical strategies for avoiding these traps. The journey begins with an overview of failure statistics and a deep dive into why these numbers remain persistently high. Subsequent chapters focus on specific causes—market demand, planning, finance, pricing, marketing, management, human resources, competition, location, adaptation, scaling, compliance, external shocks and exit strategies. By the end, you will have a clearer picture of how to start, grow, scale and eventually exit your business on your own terms and with the highest level of potential success as possible.

Whether you are a first-time entrepreneur dreaming of launching a company, a seasoned business owner looking to scale sustainably, or a consultant coaching smaller enterprises looking to scale, this book aims to be a companion on your journey. The evidence and insights presented here will help you make informed decisions, build resilience and create a business that thrives in the long run.

BONUS

As an added bonus, Eric and My Biz Coaches are launching a new assessment and application, the My Biz Navigator™ App. To support the introduction of the 7 Core Competencies and the 8 Phases of Scale along with the intersection of how they provide significant insight into where a business owner should be focused in their business throughout the lifecycle of the business.

Be sure to look for the introduction and the link to the app at the end of the book, so you can test it and apply it for yourself.

Section I

Failure Epidemic

Chapter 1

Welcome to Entrepreneurship

Four Stories No One Brags About

Every failure I've ever studied, or experienced, started the same way.

Not with bankruptcy papers. Not with a locked door. Not with a $2 million loss. It started with small blind spots.

Subtle gaps.
Rationalizations.
"It's fine."
"We'll fix it next quarter."
"That's just how business is."
"We don't have time to fix that right now."

These are four stories. Different industries. Different personalities. Different revenue levels. Same root problem. The stories have been adjusted from my clients exact scenarios, however, all of the information shared are real experiences from clients we address and work with every week. That is with the exception of story # 4 as that is my personal story of growing and building my trucking business and the amazing rise and unfortunate fall we experienced in record time.

Story #1: "They Should Know"

His firm was comfortably in the Optimizer Phase ($3M - $10M). Very profitable and regularly busy. He is well known in his market yet constantly irritated.

"My employees just don't work hard."
"They don't take initiative."

"They should know what to do."
"Why don't they work as hard as I do?"

He walked into the office every morning already frustrated. Jobs were getting done. Just not the way he wanted. Margins were tightening. Rework was increasing. Customers were mildly dissatisfied but not enough to leave.

His complaint?

"They don't do what they're supposed to."

So, I asked him a simple question:

"Have you clearly defined what 'right' looks like?"

"They should know, they've worked here for years."

"Ah, yes, but who trained them, certainly not you? So, how do you know that they know for certain?"

"Well, they should just know."

Let this enlighten you if you are misled to believe this is. No, sorry, that is not how it works.

No documented processes.
No written KPIs.
No defined quality standards.
No measurable expectations.
No consistent work review process to identify what right looks like.

You may have annual reviews, you may share when you aren't happy, but if you complain about performance, and then never directly provide guidance on how to improve, you are not leading, you aren't even being a good manager. You're simply expecting things to work themselves out, and that just doesn't happen.

He believed leadership meant intensity. It doesn't. Leadership means clarity.

His team wasn't lazy. They were guessing. And guessing creates inconsistency. Inconsistency erodes margin. Margin erosion kills scale. Documented expectations, implemented scorecards, defined roles, and installed accountability rhythms, would change everything.

Unfortunately, the business had been doing "well enough", "long enough" that the need to change didn't feel necessary. Besides, the business had operated this way for years, "it must not be that bad"…

Well, that's true, the reality is, once your business has reached a certain level of success the sense of urgency does wane a bit, in fact, it almost disappears. So much so that the owner couldn't even hear his own arrogance with the statement. The truth is that a certain amount of success can be comparable to taking a pain killer. You may not feel the immediate pain when taking the pills, but the underlying issue is still there.

If you have reached this level of success in your business but find yourself stuck and not growing significantly from that level for any extended period of time, know that the business has reached your maximum level of business competency.

And, what got you this far, will not take you to the next level, whatever that next level is. To take this business from the Optimizer Phase to the Executive Phase, one thing in particular would need to happen. This owner would need to step away from much of the day-to-day management of the firm and hire or promote someone to be Director of Operations or Chief Operating Officer.

Someone to manage the people component of the business which is not a strong competency of the owner and ultimately will affect the team, impact employee satisfaction, and potentially cause regression long term.

Now, understand, at no time did I, or would I suggest that the weaker competency of the owner in people management reflects negatively on the owner. It is simply a recognition point. This is a skill that was strong enough to take the organization to this point, however, it would be the weaker link going forward and keep the company from reaching the next phase of scale, without making this necessary change.

It's not a failure, it's an acknowledgement. As the owner and founder, you are empowered to bring in someone who is better suited to do that particular job. Allowing you to focus on the things that are even more important at this phase of scale. The challenge often is working through ego and other barriers that are prevalent when learning to work with and through others to achieve a common goal.

Could this owner, take leadership development courses, get training, and learn to be a better leader? Sure, but at this phase of scale, why would you, if you have the resources, hire someone who is better trained or prepared to do the role and allow them to do it. I spent years of my professional career doing the jobs that other owners did not want to do, or better put, realized their time was better spent on other more important components of the business, assuming I am capable of delivering the intended results.

Will there be potential growing pains? Yes, most assuredly there will be, but you don't grow without pain. And in a scenario like this one, after these many years of relative success, this owner and organization, were likely comfortable where they are in the phases of scale. However, that is good until it no longer is, and then it just might be too late.

Many people reading this right now, may be asking what's so bad about making a million or two per year? Well, nothing, until you realize you have not created real legacy value. You see a business that is solely centered around the owner this way is one bad experience from no longer being a viable business. The incapacity of the owner would completely cripple this business and likely end the operations within a year or less.

So, how many people are relying on this organization for their livelihood and how many of them, if they understand that one fact, might consider moving to another company where their future has some contingency plans built in. This is a powerful reason why small businesses often struggle to retain or hire great staff, because the owner thinks like a small business owner and not someone who is looking out for the entire organization and all its stakeholders (which does include the employees).

Story #2: "We Just Need More Leads"

This next situation, the business is in the Operator Phase ($250K to $500K) on the verge of leaping up and pushing to $1 million. They are in the professional services industry and are growing nicely, but to make the leap that they are looking for, they need to step up sales in a big way. Leads are expensive and they need to uncover a way to get more leads. Sales are soft from time to time, however, if they "just had more leads," they could make the leap they were looking for.

When I first spoke to her, she was convinced the issue was marketing.

"We just need more leads."
"If we had better advertising, this would take off."
"Our market is slow."

Her close rate?

9.7%.

"Well, that's not a lead problem. That's a conversion problem."

We walked through the numbers.

- No defined sales script
- No qualification process
- No structured follow-up
- No CRM discipline
- No targeted messaging
- Generic advertising trying to appeal to everyone

In other words, the issue wasn't volume.

It was precision.

Her marketing was broad. Her sales process was inconsistent. Her follow-up was reactive, at best. She didn't need 100 more leads. She needed to convert 25% of the ones she already had, and we would likely triple sales.

We rebuilt the sales process:

- Defined ICP (Ideal Client Profile)
- Structured a discovery process
- Developed and trained on objection handling and scripting
- Created a 7-touch follow-up automation
- Instituted conversion tracking

Within 90 days, close rate moved from 9.7% to 17%, another 4 months and we were pushing almost 28%

Same leads, mostly. Same marketing solutions, just a better message and a far better sales system. Cash flow went from stabilized to thriving, and they blew past the $1 million mark with 2 months before the end of the year.

The lesson?

Sales & Marketing without process is noise. Process turns noise into revenue. The key to success in this scenario was that the owner was convinced they should be doing better and was willing to admit they didn't know what they didn't know. That allowed me to accelerate the process and help them get impact quickly.

Story #3: "There's Just Not Enough Time"

He had just moved from the Hustler Phase to the Operator Phase and was exhausted. His business is in the home services trade and he's not quite a 1-man band, but not too much more. The wife does operations, he has one other technician, and they are all working on borrowed time holding things together with duct tape and little glue.

He did most everything and it showed.

- Sales
- Field operations
- Billing
- Collections
- Hiring
- Customer service

- Bookkeeping
- Scheduling

His business owned him. He kept saying, "I just need more time."

No. you need systems.

We recommended three simple solutions:

1. Implement automations for scheduling and invoicing

    This was relatively simple using the software we promote to our clients, we could set up AI voice automations to take calls when he wasn't available to answer, and it even could schedule appointments electronically.

    This would also allow him to initiate estimates for the work and convert them into invoices that would get paid and then allow the client to schedule the work on the calendar.

2. Hire a part-time virtual assistant

    The wife was not very good at the administrator role and actually was part of the problem. She, not only wasn't good, but she also didn't want to do that work, so he was paying her a salary, despite having to do much of the work anyway.

    We recommended adjusting the wife's role to actually do sales and marketing as that was more of her comfort anyway. We then suggested hiring a

VA (virtual assistant) who would handle the backend operations and programing for the software. The cost was almost a 3rd of the wife's salary, and the VA and automations would replace all of the work that the wife was doing and half of what the owner was doing as well.

3. This would free up his wife to do more sales and marketing, while he would have time to conduct the estimations faster, increasing client acquisition speed and give himself and the technician the bandwidth to likely increase capacity by as much as 50%.

Investment required: Modest, our services, the software and a VA at 25 hours and $12 per hour would have equated to about $2,500 per month and proposed revenue increase was likely to be no less than $15K per month without doing any marketing, just leveraging word of mouth, networking, referrals, and increased capacity. That would be a $30K investment to about $180K return of revenue, conservatively.

ROI potential: 6X

He declined. "I'll just push through this season." He kept doing everything himself.

Mistakes increased.
Invoices went out late.
Cash flow tightened.
Clients complained about delays.
Burnout set in.

Within 11 months, he shut the business down and went back to work for someone else. Not because he wasn't capable. Because he refused to stop being the bottleneck and was unwilling to leverage technology. At certain revenue levels, grit stops being an asset and starts being a liability.

Operational Excellence and Innovation and Technology are not optional.

Story #4: My Trucking Company

This one is mine. I must own the story and what it cost me. $2 million to fully understand the valuable lesson.

I started with about $150K in cash and $75K in credit. The business scaled fast. Very fast. We didn't have a problem getting business really, I did however, have a challenge getting equipment to support the growth.

As many things that my team and I did right, I made a few costly mistakes and one strategic error in estimating my skills.

We grew from startup to over $6 million in revenue annually in less than a year.

The systems were solid.
Dispatch was tight.
Processes were documented.
We had customers.

We had great contracts.
We had momentum.

We had our fair share of challenges, but we found creative ways to solve them. Finding solutions was our mantra and my knowledge and ability to understand things quickly certainly made for significant advantages. For instance, I had a business plan and clear strategy on how we would carve out a competitive advantage in the industry. One that had been around for about 100 years. I know it was a bit lofty, but I saw the potential.

A low-tech industry ripe for strong systems and processes, financial acumen, and equally strong leadership with someone who was smart and wouldn't take "no" for an answer. Without sounding arrogant, there was little I could see tripping us up. The business was a much tighter margin industry than I expected with lots of variable expenses that are not exceptionally easy to manage as you are at the whim of your drivers, unless you have great systems. That was a key component at the core of our strengths.

We negotiated to work a deal with a friend and mentor to allow us to use a seldom used 5th wheel trailer at the truck depot to act as our base of operations. We worked in it during the day and then converted the kitchen table and sofa into beds at night. We were lean and worked long and hard, my core team came to the office on Mondays and went home Friday. Two of my guys lived in San Diego, I lived in Phoenix, and the rest of my staff lived around El Centro, CA, where we based our business. A regional trucking hub for loads going to and coming from Mexico.

We went from 3 to 8 to 11 trucks by May 2018. We then hit 17 trucks by July, 23 by September, and 27 by October, by November we had exceeded $550K for the month's billings. We were growing very quickly, but nothing is inexpensive in that industry and buying trucks is no easy task, particularly when you reach over $1 million in debt on your personal credit and the companies won't loan you any more to buy trucks despite closing a deal that equates to $1.1 million annually. I thought I could use that contract to leverage the financing company to make the deal – No Deal.

We had to find a way to get 6 more trucks, so I used some creative financing options. These options included leveraging high-term interest short-term debt, loans referred to as MCA's (Merchant Cash Advance). I knew I would eventually need to bring on an investor if we intended to grow to the goal of 100 trucks. However, I figured the more we did on our own before we had to face that inevitable truth the more equity, I'd be able to keep for myself and my team that got us there. These loans would help bridge the gap to get there, that plan ended up being the mistake that took down the business.

Despite the fact that I'm actually really pretty good at math and I understood my numbers, these calculations were the leading cause of the demise. The issue was I had to take on high-interest debt to finance the down payments on the trucks. I figured we could carry the cashflow shortage for 60 days, while we got the trucks up and running, once the short-term debt was paid off on the truck(s), they would bring between $25K to $28K per month. So, as long as we kept the trucks on the road and producing with about 85% of capacity, we were good. That just didn't leave much room for error. It was a calculated gamble, but a gamble, none the less.

The issue was sustaining that level of 85% capacity. With repairs, driver shortages, increasing fuel prices...Well, you get the idea, a slower than normal holiday saw us drop by $65K in December and another $185K in January putting capacity at around 55% for the whole fleet. By February, despite capacity getting back to 70%, the damage was done and I was left with the consequence of defaulting on my first short-term loan. Then a second in March and before I knew it, I was taking high interest loans just to cover regular expenses. A sign of major challenges.

In the end, by summer 2019, I had to shut the whole operation down. Because I was too highly leveraged no one would consider helping us refinance the debt. The second major mistake I made was realizing how hard it would be to find an investor and what that process looked like. There was little about running a business I hadn't done, but raising capital was one area I had no experience in and attempted to teach myself. We no longer had the resources to hire the right people to help in this area and it proved to be a far more challenging task than I ever anticipated. Once we got upside down, everyone treated us like we had a disease and no one wanted to help us.

I can't say I blame them in retrospect, but from where we were sitting, a 3-year loan to refinance a few hundred thousand in debt and extra cash to fund the next 10 trucks would allow our business to stabilize at that size. This looked to me like a $10 million operation on the verge of scaling to 100 trucks in next 3 years, however, no one else could see that vision through all the debt but us, maybe even just me. Was I diluted with my dreams of success, maybe, but I was quickly brought back to reality with a $2.2 million dollar haircut that took me quite a few years to rebound from.

Some inevitable truths that were learned:

Growth requires capital.
Equipment isn't cheap.

Capital, or even just access to capital, can be very expensive when you need it most.
Drivers need payroll every week.
Diesel doesn't wait for receivables.

Debt was manageable… until it wasn't.

Productivity slowed slightly.
Margins tightened.
Muphy's law kicked in and, BOOM!

When you're highly leveraged, pressure compounds, FAST.

Cash can be used to create opportunity as can debt, each has an ROI, however, one of them comes at a cost. The higher that cost the more risk you have to adjust for.

The systems were there.
The hustle was there.
The leadership was there.

But Financial Acumen under aggressive growth? That lesson came the hard way. I was not only the CEO, I was also the CFO, I was good at both roles but at the size and scale, not for both roles simultaneously.

We had grown beyond our capital structure.

And when the slowdown hit, we didn't have the reserves or margin cushion to absorb it. Eventually, the weight of debt and cash flow pressure forced the shutdown. Over $2 million in losses.

It wasn't incompetence. It was imbalance and maybe a bit of arrogance. Growth without adequate financial buffers is fragility disguised as success. That whole experience reshaped how I teach scale.

Now I emphasize:

- Margin discipline
- Capital strategy
- Conservative leverage
- Scenario forecasting
- Downturn planning

Because I've lived the alternative, it wasn't pleasant, it was downright ugly!

The Pattern Behind All Four Stories

Different industries. Different revenue bands. Different personalities.

But every story exposes the same truth: Business failure is rarely caused by one catastrophic event.

It's caused by neglected competencies.

- Leadership without clarity
- Sales without structure
- Operations without systems
- Growth without capital discipline

- Hustle without leverage

In every case, the business wasn't broken. It was incomplete. And incomplete businesses don't scale.

They stall.
Or strain.
Or implode.

This is why the framework matters.

This is why the 7 Core Competencies exist. Because business doesn't fail in dramatic explosions. It fails in quiet imbalances. And if you're honest, you can probably see pieces of yourself in each one of these stories. That's not criticism. It's an invitation. Because once you can see the gaps, you can fix them.

And fixing them is how you move from statistic…
to sustainable scale.

Chapter 2

Understanding Small Business Failure

The harsh realities of entrepreneurship

Entrepreneurship is often portrayed as a path to freedom and wealth, yet the realities are sobering. The Bureau of Labor Statistics notes that nearly 25% of private-sector businesses fail within the first year[1]. After five years, nearly half have closed their doors, and after ten years roughly 70 % have failed[2]. These survival rates fluctuate by industry; for instance, information businesses have a one-year failure rate of 27.6 % and a five-year failure rate of 60.9 %[13], while agriculture and real estate firms fare better. Understanding that failure is common, sets the stage for realistic planning.

Failure rates also vary by geography. A 2025 LendingTree study found that Minnesota, the District of Columbia and Missouri have the highest first-year failure rates—27.7 %, 27.2 % and 27.1 %, respectively[14]. In contrast, Washington state exhibits the lowest first-year failure rate at 13.6 %, followed by California and Iowa[15]. Location influences business success through regulatory environments, cost structures, taxation and consumer behavior. Entrepreneurs might consider these regional variations when selecting where to open.

Beyond the numbers: Why businesses fail

Statistics describe the scale of failure but do not explain why. A deep dive into research reveals a cluster of recurring causes:

- **Insufficient market demand:** Studies show that around 35% of startups fail because there is no genuine need for their product or service[16]. Entrepreneurs often fall in love with an idea without validating whether customers will pay for it.
    - Additionally, I would add that although you may be entering a crowded market, that is not a certainty of failure, because you may be able to clearly identify your Market Dominating Position or Unique Selling Proposition (USP) in your marketing efforts and steal market share away from other longer standing competitors. However, know this is not for the faint of heart and requires even more constitution and planning to improve your odds of success.
- **Cash-flow problems:** Service Corps of Retired Executives (SCORE) reports that 82% of small businesses fail due to cash-flow issues[3]. Running out of money can result from slow sales, overexpansion, poor budgeting or inadequate funding, along with a plethora of other reasons, both external and internal.
    - Here are a few other sobering statistics, as it relates to cashflow. Most businesses start completely underfunded and nearly guarantee their unlikelihood of success from the beginning. More than 35% of businesses start with less than $5,000, no wonder the odds of financial challenges are so high. That doesn't leave much room for any margin of error.
    - Additionally, almost 73% of businesses start with less than $50,000, and of all privately started

businesses they begin with, on average, approximately $69,000.

- **Poor planning:** Experts argue that lack of planning is the underlying reason most small businesses fail[12]. Without a clear business plan, owners may underestimate costs, misjudge timelines and neglect critical tasks. All real challenges and threats to a business startup.
- **Inadequate marketing:** The U.S. Chamber of Commerce notes that 22% of failed businesses did not implement the correct marketing strategy[17]. Even the best product cannot sell if customers are unaware of it.
    - A common reason that we have discovered is that due to the lack of startup funding, most businesses do not allocate enough resources to have a marketing campaign. Instead opting to leverage referrals and word-of-mouth, however, as most experienced entrepreneurs know, those solutions don't scale as effectively as we would all like to believe.
- **Weak management and team issues:** Poor management and team problems account for nearly 20% of startup failures[11]. Visionary founders may lack managerial skills or struggle to delegate effectively.
    - In our insights over the last 6 plus years, I might suggest this is a bigger factor than the statistics might lead us to believe. What we find in many service-based businesses, particularly, the owners are quite good, even exceptional at their chosen skill or trait. However, that seldom extends into competent business management, causing numerous challenges in leadership and team management.

    - This often extends to delegating effectively, holding team members accountable, having challenging conversations, effective selection and hiring procedures and other people related challenges.
- **Overexpansion:** Growing too quickly can overstretch resources and lead to cash-flow crises[18]. Without proper systems, rapid growth becomes unsustainable.
- **External shocks and competition:** Businesses can fail because of supply-chain disruptions, economic downturns, intense competition and regulatory changes[19]. Entrepreneurs must anticipate and prepare for these forces.
    - Maybe even more recently than ever, this seems to be a larger contributing factor to the challenges that exist for business owners. We can simply look back over the last 25 years and see as many as 5 major or national contributing factors, think COVID, Housing Crisis, 9/11. Even a severe market correction can deter discretionary spending and cause 20% or more adjustments in a small business. Additionally, there have been a series of even more, smaller or regional factors that often affect the local small business owners and their ability to be successful. Consider droughts, hurricanes, flooding, wildfires, well, you get the idea.

These causes are interconnected. For example, poor planning often leads to cash-flow problems because owners underestimate how much capital they need to sustain operations. Lack of market research results in low demand, causing revenue shortfalls that trigger cash-flow crises. Inadequate marketing compounds the problem by leaving potential customers unaware of the product, while weak management makes it difficult to pivot or correct mistakes.

Learning from failure

Failure provides valuable lessons. Many successful entrepreneurs have experienced at least a few failed ventures and used those experiences to refine their strategies. Recognizing patterns of failure helps new entrepreneurs avoid repeating mistakes and encourages them to adopt practices that increase resilience. Some key lessons include:

1. **Validate your idea:** Before investing heavily in a business, conduct thorough market research. Use surveys, focus groups and tools like Google Trends to gauge interest in your product or service[20]. Develop a minimum viable product (MVP) and test it with real customers to gather feedback[21].
2. **Create a robust business plan:** A well-thought-out plan outlines your goals, target market, competitive analysis, pricing strategy, marketing, operations and financial projections[22]. It helps you anticipate challenges and ensures you remain focused.
3. **Secure adequate funding:** Do not underestimate how much capital you need to sustain the business until it becomes profitable. Explore multiple financing options, including loans, grants and investors[23]. Building cash reserves can buffer against slow periods[24]. Get access to as much as you can before you need it and be uber

disciplined with what you have because it's never enough – Real Talk.

4. **Invest in marketing:** Allocate sufficient resources to marketing and brand development. Identify your market segment and tailor your approach[25]. Track metrics such as website traffic and customer acquisition cost to refine strategies. Another big miss for founders, thinking this is where they will skimp, this slows growth and strangles can flow as sales don't ramp quickly enough.
5. **Develop leadership skills:** Recognize your strengths and limitations. Bring in experienced managers or advisors if necessary[26]. Promote a healthy workplace culture and invest in employee training[27]. Another huge missed opportunity, choosing to see it as a cost that's not necessary early on. However, this is exactly why your business will stall and teams will underperform.
6. **Scale sustainably:** Grow at a pace your infrastructure can support. Monitor cash-flow and performance metrics to avoid overexpansion[18].
7. **Prepare for external shocks:** Diversify suppliers, maintain emergency funds and monitor industry trends to adapt quickly when circumstances change[19].

The opportunity in resilience

While the failure rate is high, these figures also indicate that many businesses succeed. Roughly half of companies make it past five years[2], and around one-quarter to one-third survive beyond a decade. Those that endure tend to exhibit common traits: They solve a real problem, have strong business models, manage money prudently, invest in marketing and innovation and build adaptable organizational cultures. By studying both failures and successes, entrepreneurs gain a balanced perspective and a better chance of joining the survivors.

The subsequent chapters examine each major factor contributing to business failure in greater detail. They provide frameworks, tools and real-world examples to help entrepreneurs navigate the complexities of starting and running a successful business.

Chapter 3

Market Research and Demand: Is There a Need?

The centrality of market need

One of the first questions any entrepreneur should ask is "does anyone actually need what I'm offering?" Numerous studies show that lack of market need is a primary reason for business failure. The U.S. Chamber of Commerce notes that nearly 35% of startups fail because there is insufficient demand for their product or service[16]. Capsule CRM's analysis echoes this, highlighting that many founders set up a business first and figure out whom they sell to second, leading to a mismatch between product and market[28].

Entrepreneurs often assume that their idea is unique or that passion alone will drive success. However, the market determines whether an idea has value. Without customers who are willing and able to pay for your product or service, even the most innovative concept will struggle. To avoid this fate, prospective business owners must invest in thorough market research before launching.

Tools and techniques for market research

Primary research: Collecting data directly from potential customers gives insight into their preferences, pain points and willingness to pay. Methods include surveys, interviews and focus groups. Surveys can measure potential demand, price sensitivity and desired features. Interviews allow deeper exploration of customer motivations. Focus groups provide dynamic discussions where participants build on each other's comments.

Secondary research: Secondary sources include market reports, industry statistics, academic studies, competitor websites and government databases. Resources like Google Trends can reveal how often people search for keywords related to your product or service[29]. Trade associations and government agencies, such as the Small Business Administration and Bureau of Labor Statistics, publish industry trends and demographic data that help estimate market size.

Customer persona development: Creating detailed profiles of your ideal customers, based on demographics, psychographics, behaviors and motivations, helps you tailor your offering. For example, a persona for an eco-friendly cleaning product might include environmentally conscious parents aged 30–45 with middle-to-high income levels.

Competitive analysis: Evaluate competitors' offerings, pricing, strengths and weaknesses. Determine where your product fits in the market and how you can differentiate. Tools like SWOT analysis (strengths, weaknesses, opportunities and threats) help identify competitive gaps and potential threats. Recognize that 20% of businesses fail because they cannot keep up with competition[30], so identifying your unique selling proposition (USP) is critical.

Validating your idea: The minimum viable product

Many founders rush to build a full product without testing assumptions. Developing a minimum viable product (MVP), a simplified version of your offering with core features, allows you to test market response with minimal investment. CapsuleCRM encourages entrepreneurs to validate their ideas through an MVP before committing significant resources[31]. By releasing an MVP, you can collect real customer feedback, refine your value proposition and pivot if necessary.

Lean methodology advocates iterative cycles: Build, measure, learn. After releasing the MVP, track metrics like conversion rates, retention and customer satisfaction. Use the data to improve the product and adjust marketing messages. This process reduces risk and ensures you are building something the market truly wants.

Understanding customer willingness to pay

Even if customers need your solution, they may not pay for it if it's priced incorrectly. Conduct pricing research through surveys asking prospective customers what they would pay and through experiments like A/B testing different price points. The FibreCU article stresses that overpricing or underpricing can harm your business, and rebuilding demand can be difficult[32]. Use cost-plus, value-based or competitive pricing strategies to set initial prices, and remain flexible to adjust as you learn more.

Adapting to changing demand

Customer preferences evolve. What solves a problem today may be obsolete tomorrow. Companies that thrive monitor trends, track changes in consumer behavior and adapt quickly. The U.S. Chamber of Commerce suggests hiring creative, forward-thinking employees and researching what's trending to stay relevant[33].

For example, the rise of streaming services disrupted DVD rental stores, but companies that pivoted to digital platforms survived.

Common mistakes in market research

- **Confirmation bias:** Entrepreneurs may selectively seek information that confirms their idea. Mitigate this by deliberately looking for disconfirming evidence.
- **Overreliance on friends and family:** While feedback from friends is valuable, they may not be representative of your target market. Strive for diverse input.
- **Ignoring market size:** Even if customers love your product, the market may be too small to sustain a business. Estimate the total addressable market (TAM), serviceable addressable market (SAM) and serviceable obtainable market (SOM).
- **Neglecting competitor responses:** Competitors may quickly replicate your innovation. Evaluate how defensible your advantage is and plan accordingly.

Practical steps for entrepreneurs

1. **Define your problem:** Articulate the problem your product or service solves. Ensure it is painful enough that customers will pay to alleviate it.
2. **Map the customer journey:** Identify the steps your customer takes from becoming aware of the problem to purchasing a solution. This reveals pain points and opportunities.

3. **Conduct mixed-method research:** Use both quantitative (surveys, analytics) and qualitative (interviews, observation) methods to develop a rich understanding.
4. **Test early and often:** Create prototypes or MVPs and gather feedback. Iterate based on the data.
5. **Monitor the market:** Regularly review industry reports, competitor news and consumer trends. Stay attuned to changes that may affect demand.

By rigorously validating demand and continuously monitoring the market, entrepreneurs avoid the trap of building products that nobody wants. The next chapter builds on this foundation by showing how to translate research into a coherent business plan.

Chapter 4

Crafting a Solid Business Plan

Why planning matters

Business plans are more than formal documents for investors; they are roadmaps that guide decision-making. Studies show that lack of planning is the underlying reason many businesses fail[12]. Without a plan, owners may underestimate costs, misallocate resources and drift away from their goals. Plans enforce discipline by requiring entrepreneurs to research their market, articulate objectives and outline strategies.

Investopedia stresses that a solid and realistic business plan forms the basis of a successful business[34]. The Small Business Administration offers templates that include sections on description, organizational structure, market analysis, marketing and sales strategies and financial projections[35]. While plans vary by industry and stage, they share core elements that ensure clarity and accountability.

Key components of an effective business plan

1. **Executive summary:** Provide a concise overview of your business, including the mission, products or services, target market and financial highlights. The summary should capture the reader's attention and convey the essence of the enterprise.

2. **Company description:** Detail your company's history (if any), structure, ownership and vision. Explain what sets the business apart from competitors.
3. **Market analysis:** Summarize your research on industry trends, market size, customer segments and competition. Use data from credible sources like government reports, trade associations and academic studies to support your analysis.
4. **Organization and management:** Outline the organizational structure, roles and responsibilities. Identify key team members and their qualifications. If you plan to hire fractional executives or consultants, as the U.S. Chamber suggests when budgets are limited[26], explain their roles.
5. **Products or services:** Describe your offerings, emphasizing their benefits and how they meet customer needs. Highlight intellectual property, proprietary technologies or competitive advantages.
6. **Marketing and sales strategies:** Explain how you will reach customers and convert them into paying clients. Discuss branding, pricing, distribution channels and promotional tactics. Identify metrics for evaluating effectiveness, as recommended by marketing experts[25].
7. **Financial plan:** Present projected income statements, cash-flow statements and balance sheets. Include assumptions behind revenue forecasts and expense estimates. Discuss funding requirements, potential investors or lenders and how you will use funds.
8. **Risk management and contingency plans:** Identify potential risks, such as supply-chain disruptions, regulatory changes or economic downturns, and outline mitigation

strategies. This shows investors that you are prepared for uncertainties.

9. **Appendices:** Provide supporting documents, such as resumes of key personnel, market research reports, legal agreements and technical specifications.

How to write and revise your plan

Research thoroughly: A credible plan requires accurate data. Use reliable sources like the U.S. Bureau of Labor Statistics, Small Business Administration and industry reports. Cite statistics such as failure rates (e.g., 49.9 % of businesses fail within five years[2]) to highlight the importance of proper planning. Industry benchmarks help you make realistic financial projections.

Set SMART goals: Goals should be Specific, Measurable, Achievable, Relevant and Time-bound. For example, "Achieve $500,000 in revenue by the end of year two by acquiring 1,000 customers with an average order value of $500."

Align your plan with your values: The mission and vision statements should reflect why you started the business. Authenticity resonates with customers and employees, fostering loyalty.

Seek feedback: Share your draft plan with mentors, advisors or potential investors. They can identify weaknesses, unrealistic assumptions or overlooked risks. The Georgia SBDC stresses the value of consulting mentors and business associations[36].

Update regularly: Business plans are living documents. Review and adjust them as market conditions change or as you learn more through experience. Update financial projections, marketing strategies and risk assessments at least annually.

Common planning mistakes

- **Overly optimistic projections:** Founders often underestimate expenses and overestimate revenue. Use conservative assumptions and include contingencies.
- **Ignoring competitors:** Failing to account for competitive responses leads to unrealistic market share estimates. Regularly monitor competitor activity and adjust your strategy accordingly.
- **Lack of risk analysis:** Many plans ignore external threats like regulatory changes, natural disasters or supply-chain disruptions. Identify potential risks and develop contingency plans.
- **Static planning:** Treating the business plan as a one-time exercise rather than a dynamic tool leads to outdated strategies. Revisit and revise the plan regularly.

Leveraging your plan to secure funding

Investors and lenders require a well-structured plan to evaluate the viability of your business. They look for evidence of market demand, a compelling value proposition, a capable management team and a realistic path to profitability. Highlight credible statistics—such as the 82 % failure due to cash-flow issues[3] or the 35 % failure due to lack of market demand[16]—to show you understand the risks and have strategies to mitigate them. Show

how your plan addresses these risks through solid research, conservative financial projections and contingency plans.

Adapting your plan for different stages

Business plans evolve as companies grow. Early-stage plans focus on market research, product development and funding needs. Growth-stage plans emphasize scaling operations, expanding into new markets and refining marketing strategies. Mature companies planning an exit, need plans that address succession, sale or IPO. The final chapters of this book provide guidance on exit planning, but your initial business plan should already anticipate how you might eventually exit, as this affects how you structure ownership and make decisions.

In summary, a robust business plan is both a map and a compass. It forces you to articulate assumptions, set goals and prepare for uncertainties. By investing time and effort in crafting and updating your plan, you reduce the likelihood of failure and increase your chances of attracting investors, lenders and talented team members.

I'll add this as it relates to creating a business plan. As much value as the plan itself can have, the action of challenging yourself to go through this process before diving in will have a significant impact in your ability to sustain in business longer than most. Which is often all it might take to truly succeed.

Things like how to plan for the inevitable challenges that will come up – cashflow issues, sales slumps, mistakes, poor calculations, slow paying clients, and a host of other concerns that will test your business. You'll have the ability to create solutions in a safe space with a clear mind without the disrupted energy of stress and anxiety.

I can't even begin to explain all the benefits that this process provides, so I'll leave you with this. No matter how much you think you know about this new endeavor, just remember this phrase: "You don't know, what you don't know, and right now you don't know shit. As a matter of fact, when you realize that you don't know anything, you'll realize something that's very important."

Be willing to hold to that mantra and your life as an entrepreneur will be astronomically better!

When unconscious incompetence slowly becomes conscious incompetence, that's progress. When unconscious competence kicks in, things are getting good and by the time you've actually reached conscious competence, you are likely quite older, but also realized things have changed and there are now new things you are not entirely competent in…

To be a successful entrepreneur, you must commit to being a life-long learner.

Chapter 5

Financing and Cashflow Management

Cashflow: The lifeblood of business

Cashflow, the movement of money into and out of your business, is the lifeblood of any enterprise. Without adequate cash, a profitable company can still fail because it cannot pay its bills, compensate employees or invest in growth. SCORE's research reveals that 82 % of small businesses fail due to cash-flow problems[3]. Cashflow issues often stem from deeper problems such as undercapitalization, poor budgeting, overinvestment in inventory or slow collection of receivables.

Estimating capital requirements

One of the biggest mistakes new entrepreneurs make is underestimating how much money they need to start and sustain their business. Georgia's SBDC highlights that many owners underestimate costs and how long it will take to become profitable[37]. To estimate capital requirements:

1. **Calculate startup costs:** List one-time expenses such as equipment, legal fees, licenses, renovations and initial inventory. Factor in deposits for rent and utilities.
2. **Forecast operating expenses:** Estimate monthly expenses for rent, payroll, utilities, marketing, insurance, supplies and taxes. Be conservative and include a buffer for unforeseen costs.

3. **Project revenue:** Based on market research, estimate sales volume and average transaction value. Consider seasonality and ramp-up time. Recognize that revenue may start slowly and build over months or years.
4. **Determine working capital needs:** Working capital equals current assets minus current liabilities. Adequate working capital ensures you can cover day-to-day expenses. Many consultants recommend having at least six months of operating expenses on hand.
5. **Plan for contingencies:** Set aside cash reserves to handle emergencies, slow sales or delayed payments. SCORE advises building cash reserves so you can survive down cycles[24].

Funding options

Securing financing requires understanding the pros and cons of different sources:

- **Personal savings:** Using personal funds avoids debt and investor pressure, but it concentrates risk on the founder. Never invest money you cannot afford to lose. This often includes that retirement fund or equity in the house you were thinking of.
- **Family and friends:** These informal investors may provide flexible terms, but mixing personal relationships with business can be risky. Document agreements to avoid misunderstandings and proceed with caution on this one.
- **Bank loans:** Banks offer term loans and lines of credit. Lenders want to see a detailed business plan, good credit history and collateral. The U.S. Small Business Administration (SBA) provides loan programs for

startups[38]. These are also good an bad options, so do your due diligence and make sure you know what you are signing up for. Personal guarantees have taken down many ambitious entrepreneurs.

- **Government grants and loans:** Government agencies offer grants for specific industries or demographics. Research federal, state and local programs. Just know these take time and companies will charge sometimes as much as the grant you may get, while promising the world, do your due diligence.
- **Angel investors:** Angels are individuals who invest in early-stage companies in exchange for equity. They often provide mentorship alongside capital.
- **Venture capital:** Venture capitalists (VCs) invest in high-growth startups but require significant ownership stakes and control. VC funding is competitive and suits scalable businesses with large market opportunities.
- **Crowdfunding:** Platforms like Kickstarter and Indiegogo allow entrepreneurs to raise small amounts from many backers, often in exchange for early access or perks. Crowdfunding also tests market interest. These options have their place, but not ideal for all businesses and does require some serious "salesmanship" to get people excited about supporting your endeavor.
- **Revenue-based financing:** Some lenders provide capital in exchange for a percentage of future revenue. This structure can be attractive for businesses with predictable revenue streams. This also comes with aggressive repayment terms and often can be quite expensive, read the fine print.

Final thoughts on this topic, I have used most all of these and worked with partners or clients who have used those options that I have not. I can say this for that collective experience, which is quite vast. None of these options are ideal, and none of them are necessarily bad ideas. They all have their place.

You must identify your risk tolerance, control tolerance, and understand that a bad deal can end a friendship or strain a relationship, and so could a good or even great deal. Obviously a failed opportunity where money is lost, likely would not end well, however, if an investor feels like they got the short end of an amazing deal. That too can add immense strain.
The key is in clearly defining the expectations, documenting everything, and ensuring that regardless of how things work out, business is business and personal is personal. However, that seems to be nearly impossible for most people to practice.

Managing cash-flow

1. Monitor cash-flow regularly: Use accounting software to track cash in real time. Review cash-flow statements monthly, noting trends and anomalies.

2. Speed up receivables: Invoice customers promptly and offer incentives for early payment. For clients with long payment cycles, consider invoice factoring or negotiating shorter terms.

3. Control payables: Negotiate favorable payment terms with suppliers. Pay invoices on time to maintain good relationships and avoid late fees, but do not pay too early if it strains cash.

4. Manage inventory: Excess inventory ties up cash and risks obsolescence. SCORE notes that poor inventory management leads to unnecessary orders, expired items and backorders[39]. Use inventory management systems to track stock levels and reorder points.

5. Create a cash-flow forecast: Project cash inflows and outflows weekly or monthly. Identify periods where cash may be tight and plan accordingly. Adjust marketing campaigns or expenses to smooth cash-flow.

6. Build reserves: Maintain an emergency fund to cover three to six months of operating expenses. Reserves provide a cushion during downturns and reduce reliance on credit.

Know this about cashflow, it never seems to work the way you want and being bigger doesn't necessarily make it easier, it just comes with different types of problems. In the beginning it might be you can't pay the mortgage, then it will be payroll issues if money is short, then it is tax challenges, and eventually it might be valuation issues or any combination of those as well as others.

Remember this about managing finances in a business, you'll never feel like you have enough, however, personally, I would rather have resources and options to deal with the problems, then debating not paying my mortgage. Been there done that, not fun! Consider growing your business to at least the $1 million range and you'll likely have created more options.

Financial management systems

Investing in financial management tools and expertise is essential. Use accounting software such as QuickBooks or Xero to automate invoicing, track expenses and generate financial statements. Engage a certified public accountant (CPA) or fractional CFO if your budget allows, as recommended by the U.S. Chamber of Commerce[40]. Professional advice ensures compliance with tax regulations and helps interpret financial data.

Credit and debt management

Poor credit management can sink a business. SCORE warns against delaying payments or manipulating payment terms, as such behavior damages credit and reduces financing options[41]. Entrepreneurs should protect their credit by paying bills on time, maintaining a favorable credit utilization ratio and monitoring credit reports. When using debt:

- **Choose the right type:** Match the financing method to the purpose (e.g., short-term working capital vs. long-term asset purchase).
- **Understand the terms:** Evaluate interest rates, fees, covenants and repayment schedules. Avoid loans with burdensome covenants that restrict operations.
- **Avoid overleveraging:** Excessive debt increases risk and reduces flexibility. Calculate your debt-to-equity ratio and ensure it remains within industry norms.

Cash-flow as a strategic tool

Cash-flow management is not just about survival; it is a strategic tool. Healthy cash-flow enables you to seize opportunities, such as purchasing inventory at a discount, investing in marketing campaigns or acquiring competitors. By maintaining strong cash reserves, you strengthen your bargaining position with suppliers and lenders. Conversely, cash-flow crises force you into reactive measures like cutting staff or delaying investments, which can harm long-term prospects.

In the next chapter we will examine pricing strategies—a factor closely tied to cash-flow and profitability—and explore how businesses can set prices that cover costs, generate margins and appeal to customers.

Chapter 6

Pricing Strategies and Profitability

Why pricing matters

Pricing is more than a mathematical exercise; it signals value, influences customer perception and determines profitability. FibreCU warns that mispricing, either overpricing or underpricing, can hurt a business and that recovering from incorrect pricing is difficult[32]. Set prices too high and you deter customers; set them too low and undermine margins and brand perception. Crafting an effective pricing strategy requires balancing costs, customer willingness to pay and competitive positioning.

Understanding costs

Before setting prices, understand your costs thoroughly. Costs include direct costs (materials, labor), indirect costs (rent, utilities, insurance) and variable costs (shipping, transaction fees). Overhead allocation is often overlooked, leading to underpricing. Use accurate cost accounting to ensure each product or service covers its share of fixed and variable costs. Include allowances for returns, discounts and bad debt.

Pricing models

1. **Cost-plus pricing:** Calculate the cost of producing the product or delivering the service, then add a markup.

While simple, cost-plus may not account for customer perceptions or competitor prices.

2. **Competitive pricing:** Set prices relative to competitors. This model requires understanding your competitors' price points and value propositions. If you offer superior features or service, you may justify a premium price.
3. **Value-based pricing:** Base the price on the perceived value to the customer rather than costs. This approach is common in software, consulting and luxury goods. It requires deep insight into customer needs and willingness to pay.
4. **Dynamic pricing:** Adjust prices based on demand, time or customer segment. Airlines and ride-share companies use dynamic pricing extensively. For small businesses, dynamic pricing can be implemented through seasonal promotions, flash sales or loyalty programs.
5. **Freemium and subscription models:** Offer a basic version for free and charge for premium features. This model works well for digital products and membership services but requires careful conversion strategies.

Psychological pricing

Psychology plays a role in pricing. Examples include:

- **Charm pricing:** Pricing items at $9.99 instead of $10 taps into perceived bargain effects.
- **Price anchoring:** Displaying a high "original" price next to a discounted price makes the discount appear more attractive.

- **Decoy pricing:** Offering three options (low, mid and high) encourages customers to choose the mid-range option.
- **Bundling:** Combining multiple products or services at a single price increases perceived value.

Aligning pricing with market strategy

Pricing should align with your market positioning. If your brand emphasizes premium quality, low prices may erode credibility. Conversely, a value brand may rely on competitive pricing. Use market research to determine where your offering fits on the price-value spectrum. Recognize that price is a key component of your marketing strategy and influences how customers perceive your brand.

Monitoring and adjusting prices

Prices are not set in stone. Monitor sales volumes, margins, customer feedback and competitor actions. Use A/B testing or pilot programs to experiment with different price points. Collect data on how price changes affect demand and profitability. If costs rise due to inflation, supply-chain disruptions or regulatory changes, adjust prices accordingly. Communicate price changes transparently to customers, emphasizing value and explaining the reasons behind increases when possible.

Pricing pitfalls to avoid

- **Ignoring perceived value:** Customers buy based on perceived value, not just cost. Emphasize the benefits of your product or service.
- **Following competitors blindly:** Copying competitors' prices without analyzing your own costs and positioning can be fatal.
- **Price wars:** Engaging in price wars erodes margins and can damage the brand. Compete on value rather than price alone.
- **Failing to account for discounts and promotions:** Frequent discounts can train customers to wait for sales, reducing profitability. Plan promotional activities strategically.

In summary, pricing is both an art and a science. It requires understanding costs, customer psychology, competitive dynamics and your overall business strategy. An effective pricing strategy contributes directly to cash-flow health, profitability and long-term success.

Chapter 7

Marketing: Reaching and Engaging Customers

The importance of marketing

Marketing bridges the gap between your product and your customers. The U.S. Chamber of Commerce points out that inadequate marketing is a major reason small businesses fail; 22 % of failed businesses did not implement the correct marketing strategy[17]. Georgia's SBDC likewise notes that the best product will not sell if customers do not know about it[42]. Effective marketing builds brand awareness, generates leads and turns prospects into loyal customers.

Building a brand

A brand is more than a logo or slogan; it encompasses the personality, values and promise your business conveys. Strong brands evoke trust and emotional connections. Define your brand identity by articulating your mission, vision, values and unique selling proposition. Develop a consistent visual identity (logo, colors, typography) and tone of voice across all channels. Authentic storytelling can humanize your brand and make it more relatable.

Developing a marketing strategy

An effective marketing strategy answers three questions: who are your customers, what message will resonate with them and how will you reach them? Components include:

- **Segmentation and targeting:** Identify distinct customer segments based on demographics, behaviors and needs. Tailor messages and offers to each segment.
- **Positioning:** Clarify how you want customers to perceive your brand relative to competitors. Positioning statements should highlight your USP and the benefits customers will receive.
- **Promotion:** Select the channels—digital, traditional or a mix—that your target audience uses. Digital channels include social media, search engine marketing, content marketing, email and influencer partnerships. Traditional channels include print ads, direct mail, events and sponsorships.
- **Budgeting:** Allocate resources based on expected return on investment (ROI). Track spending and performance metrics to optimize allocation.

Digital marketing essentials

In today's environment, digital marketing is indispensable. Businesses with weak digital presence risk invisibility[43]. Key digital tactics include:

- **Search engine optimization (SEO):** Optimize your website to rank highly on search engines for relevant keywords. Use quality content, proper tags and mobile-friendly design.

- **Content marketing:** Provide valuable content (blogs, videos, podcasts, guides) that educates and entertains your target audience. Content builds trust and positions you as an authority.
- **Social media marketing:** Engage with customers on platforms like Facebook, Instagram, LinkedIn and TikTok. Use a mix of organic posts and paid ads to reach wider audiences.
- **Email marketing:** Build an email list and send personalized newsletters, promotions and updates. Email remains one of the highest ROI marketing channels.
- **Pay-per-click (PPC) advertising:** Use platforms like Google Ads and social media ads to target specific keywords or audiences. Monitor click-through rates and conversion rates to refine campaigns.
- **Analytics and tracking:** Use tools like Google Analytics and social media insights to measure traffic, engagement, conversion and ROI. Data-driven decisions improve effectiveness.

Offline marketing tactics

Offline strategies remain relevant, especially for local businesses. Consider:

- **Networking and referrals:** Attend industry events, join local business associations and ask satisfied customers for referrals.

- **Public relations:** Generate media coverage through press releases, thought leadership articles and community involvement.
- **Events and sponsorships:** Host workshops, participate in trade shows and sponsor community events to increase visibility.
- **Direct mail and print advertising:** Target local residents or specific demographics with postcards, flyers or magazine ads.

Measuring marketing success

Measure performance using metrics aligned with goals. Key indicators include:

- **Customer acquisition cost (CAC):** The average cost of acquiring a new customer. Compare CAC to customer lifetime value (CLV) to ensure profitability.
- **Conversion rate:** The percentage of prospects who take a desired action (purchase, signup). Optimize landing pages and calls-to-action to increase conversion.
- **Engagement metrics:** Likes, shares, comments, time on site and email open rates indicate how well your content resonates.
- **Return on marketing investment (ROMI):** (Revenue – Marketing cost) / Marketing cost. Aim for positive ROMI; adjust spending based on performance.

Common marketing mistakes

- **Lack of strategy:** Random marketing activities without a cohesive plan waste resources and produce inconsistent results.
- **Neglecting the target audience:** Marketing to a broad audience dilutes your message. Focus on defined segments.
- **Failure to track:** Without tracking, you cannot know which activities work. Use analytics to inform decisions.
- **Underestimating costs:** Marketing can be expensive. Budget appropriately and adjust based on results. Inadequate budgeting is a common reason for marketing failure[44].

Marketing is a vital investment, not an optional expense. A well-executed marketing strategy positions your brand, attracts customers and sustains growth. In the next chapter we will explore the human element—management and leadership—which is equally essential for success.

Chapter 8

Management and Leadership Skills

The founder's dilemma

Many entrepreneurs are visionaries passionate about their product or service. However, passion does not automatically translate into effective management. The U.S. Chamber of Commerce observes that many founders lack the attributes of a strong manager and do not have time to oversee employees[45]. As the business grows, tasks multiply, hiring, budgeting, marketing, customer service and strategy, making it impossible for one person to manage everything effectively.

Characteristics of effective leaders

Effective leaders cultivate qualities that inspire and guide teams:

- **Vision:** Articulating a clear vision helps employees understand the company's purpose and direction. Vision aligns daily tasks with long-term goals.
- **Communication:** Leaders must communicate expectations clearly and listen to employees' feedback. Transparent communication fosters trust and collaboration.
- **Empathy:** Understanding employees' perspectives builds rapport and improves morale. Empathetic leaders support work–life balance and show genuine concern for their team.

- **Adaptability:** Markets and internal circumstances change. Leaders who embrace change, learn quickly and adjust strategy maintain competitiveness.
- **Delegation:** Knowing when and how to delegate tasks prevents burnout and allows employees to contribute meaningfully. Delegation requires trust and clear instructions.
- **Decision-making:** Leaders must make timely decisions based on data, experience and intuition. Avoid analysis paralysis while ensuring due diligence.

Building a management team

Hiring a management team is challenging for cash-strapped startups. However, failing to bring in leadership help can lead to mismanagement of finances, hiring and marketing[46]. Options include:

- **Fractional executives:** Hiring a part-time chief financial officer (CFO), chief marketing officer (CMO) or chief operating officer (COO) provides expertise without the cost of full-time salaries. Fractional executives bring experience from multiple industries and can set up systems and processes.
- **Middle managers:** As the team grows, bring on mid-level managers to oversee departments. They bridge the gap between leadership and frontline staff.
- **Virtual assistants:** Virtual assistants can handle administrative tasks, freeing the founder to focus on strategic priorities.

- **Advisors and mentors:** Seek guidance from mentors, industry experts and advisory boards. They offer insight, accountability and networks.

Employee management and engagement

Poor employee management can cause high turnover, stress, low engagement and poor performance[47]. To build an engaged workforce:

- **Define roles and expectations:** Provide clear job descriptions and performance metrics. Ambiguity breeds frustration.
- **Offer training and development:** Invest in training to improve skills and confidence. Provide opportunities for career advancement.
- **Foster a positive culture:** Encourage teamwork, celebrate achievements and promote open communication. Address conflict promptly and fairly.
- **Provide feedback and recognition:** Regularly recognize good work. Constructive feedback helps employees grow and shows you care about their success.
- **Encourage autonomy:** Empower employees to make decisions within their responsibilities. Autonomy increases satisfaction and innovation.

Performance management systems

Implement performance evaluations that align with company goals. Use key performance indicators (KPIs) to measure individual and team success. Examples include sales targets, customer satisfaction scores or project completion rates. Conduct regular performance reviews to discuss achievements, challenges and development plans.

Succession planning

Planning for leadership transitions ensures continuity. Identify potential successors early and provide mentorship and training. Document processes, contacts and knowledge to reduce disruption when key leaders leave. Succession planning is also a component of exit strategies, which we discuss in Chapter 15.

Common management pitfalls

- **Micromanagement:** Hovering over employees stifles initiative and creativity. Trust your team to perform.
- **Failure to delegate:** Holding onto all decisions slows progress and leads to burnout. Delegate tasks to competent team members.
- **Ignoring employee feedback:** Employees have valuable insights into operations. Ignoring their input can lead to missed opportunities for improvement.
- **Lack of accountability:** When poor performance goes unaddressed, it demotivates high performers. Hold everyone, including leadership, accountable.

Effective management and leadership empower employees, align the organization and drive performance. Entrepreneurs who invest in developing leadership skills and building strong management teams are better equipped to navigate challenges and avoid common pitfalls. The next chapter focuses on building and nurturing a winning team.

Chapter 9

Building and Nurturing a Winning Team

The importance of the right team

Behind every successful business is a team of individuals whose skills and dedication turn vision into reality. Many startups fail because they do not have the right team; nearly 20 % of failed startups cite team problems[11]. Building a strong team involves hiring people with complementary skills, aligning them with the company's mission and fostering a culture where they can thrive.

Hiring strategies

Define roles and competencies: Begin by clearly defining the roles you need and the competencies required. Create job descriptions that specify duties, performance expectations and the skills or experience required. For example, a marketing manager may need expertise in digital marketing, copywriting and analytics.

Focus on cultural fit: Skills can be taught, but cultural fit is harder to change. Look for candidates who share your company's values and exhibit behaviors that align with your culture. Cultural fit does not mean hiring clones; it means ensuring diversity of thought and background within a shared set of core values.

Hire for potential: For early-stage companies with limited budgets, hire individuals who are adaptable and eager to learn. They may not have all the skills yet, but they possess the aptitude and attitude to grow with the business.

Use structured interviews: Structured interviews; where all candidates are asked the same questions, reduce bias and improve the reliability of hiring decisions. Include behavioral questions that assess problem-solving, teamwork and leadership.

Conduct reference checks: Speak with former employers or colleagues to verify experience, work ethic and performance.

Onboarding and training

An effective onboarding process sets new hires up for success. Provide orientation on company history, mission, culture, policies and expectations. Assign a mentor or buddy to help new employees integrate. Training should cover job-specific skills, tools, software and processes. Ensure that employees understand how their work contributes to company goals.

Developing a cohesive team

Encourage collaboration: Use cross-functional teams to break down silos and foster innovation. Collaboration encourages diverse perspectives and improves problem-solving.

Promote diversity and inclusion: Diverse teams are more creative and better reflect the customer base. Create policies that support equal opportunity and inclusive practices. Provide training on unconscious bias and anti-discrimination.

Build trust: Trust is the foundation of effective teams. Leaders build trust by being transparent, keeping commitments and treating everyone respectfully. Encourage teams to trust one another by promoting open communication and accountability.

Celebrate achievements: Recognize individual and team accomplishments. Public recognition, bonuses or small rewards boost morale and reinforce desired behaviors.

Employee retention

Recruiting new employees is costly. Retaining talent is more cost-effective and preserves institutional knowledge. To retain employees:

- **Offer competitive compensation:** Pay salaries that reflect market rates and the value employees bring. Provide benefits such as health insurance, retirement plans, paid time off and flexible work arrangements.
- **Provide career development:** Offer training, mentorship and growth opportunities. Encourage employees to pursue certifications or further education.
- **Foster a positive work environment:** Ensure that the workplace is safe, inclusive and supportive. Address toxic behaviors and resolve conflicts promptly.
- **Listen and respond:** Conduct regular engagement surveys and listen to feedback. Act on suggestions to improve the work environment.

Managing conflict

Conflict is inevitable in teams. Managed well, it can lead to constructive debate and improved decisions. Managed poorly, it causes stress and undermines trust. Leaders should:

- **Establish clear expectations:** Define acceptable behaviors and a code of conduct.
- **Address issues early:** Do not ignore signs of conflict; intervene quickly to prevent escalation.
- **Use mediation:** In complex disputes, use neutral mediators to facilitate productive conversation.
- **Encourage empathy:** Encourage team members to understand others' perspectives and find common ground.

When to part ways

Despite best efforts, some employees may not perform or fit. Holding onto underperformers can drain resources and demoralize others. Use performance improvement plans and provide opportunities for improvement. If performance does not improve, part ways respectfully and fairly. Document performance issues and follow legal procedures to avoid claims of wrongful termination.

Building and nurturing a winning team requires intentional efforts in hiring, onboarding, development, culture and retention. A cohesive, motivated team not only executes the founder's vision but also contributes ideas, identifies risks and drives innovation. The next chapter examines competition and differentiation—critical for standing out in crowded markets.

Chapter 10

Competition and Differentiation

The competitive landscape

Operating without understanding the competitive landscape is perilous. CapsuleCRM notes that approximately 20 % of businesses fail because they cannot keep up with competitors[48]. Competition can come from direct rivals offering similar products, indirect competitors offering alternative solutions and substitutes that satisfy the same customer need. To survive and thrive, businesses must differentiate themselves and deliver unique value.

Competitive analysis frameworks

SWOT analysis: Identify your internal strengths and weaknesses and external opportunities and threats. This framework helps prioritize strategic initiatives.

Porter's Five Forces: Analyze industry forces—competitive rivalry, threat of new entrants, bargaining power of suppliers, bargaining power of customers and threat of substitutes. Understanding these forces reveals where you can influence and where you must adapt.

Competitor profiling: Create profiles for key competitors, including their products, pricing, target markets, marketing strategies and strengths. Continually update these profiles as competitors evolve.

Differentiation strategies

Product differentiation: Offer features, quality or design that competitors do not. For example, a bakery may differentiate with organic ingredients or gluten-free options.

Price differentiation: Compete on cost by offering similar value at a lower price, or command a premium by offering superior value. Price differentiation must align with your brand and financial model.

Service differentiation: Provide exceptional customer service, personalized experiences or faster delivery. Zappos built a strong brand by prioritizing customer service.

Brand differentiation: Develop a distinctive brand identity that resonates with customers. A compelling story, visual identity and voice can set you apart even if the product is similar.

Channel differentiation: Use unique distribution channels. Direct-to-consumer (DTC) brands differentiate by selling online and bypassing traditional retail.

Innovation: Introduce new technologies, processes or business models. Companies like Netflix revolutionized media consumption by shifting from DVD rentals to streaming.

Strategies for staying competitive

- **Continuous improvement:** Adopt a culture of ongoing improvement. Encourage employees to identify inefficiencies and propose solutions.

- **Customer focus:** Understand customer needs and deliver experiences that exceed expectations. Loyal customers can become brand advocates, giving you an edge over competitors.
- **Agility:** Respond quickly to market changes. Develop flexible processes that allow you to pivot when necessary.
- **Strategic partnerships:** Collaborate with complementary businesses to expand your offering or reach. Partnerships can amplify strengths and offset weaknesses.
- **Invest in innovation:** Allocate resources to research and development. Experiment with new products or services, and use feedback loops to iterate.

Avoiding competitive traps

- **Copying competitors:** While it is important to learn from competitors, simply imitating them does not create differentiation. Use competitor insights to identify gaps in the market rather than replicate existing offerings.
- **Neglecting core competencies:** Focus on what you do best. Diversifying into unrelated areas can dilute your brand and resources.
- **Competing solely on price:** Price wars erode margins and may not be sustainable. Compete on value and build brand loyalty instead.

Monitoring the competitive environment

Set up systems to track competitor activity. Use Google Alerts, industry newsletters, social media monitoring and customer feedback. Encourage employees to share information about competitor promotions, product launches and customer reactions. Use this data to refine your strategy and maintain a competitive advantage.

By understanding the competitive landscape and differentiating effectively, entrepreneurs can carve out a distinctive place in the market and reduce the risk of being outperformed. The next chapter explores how location and digital presence shape accessibility and customer acquisition.

Chapter 11

Location and Digital Presence

The impact of physical location

Location influences foot traffic, accessibility, cost and the overall success of a business. Investopedia highlights that poor location can hamper businesses dependent on foot traffic[49]. For example, a retail store tucked away on a side street may struggle to attract customers compared to one on a busy avenue. Entrepreneurs must evaluate accessibility, visibility, parking and proximity to suppliers and competitors when choosing a location.

Online presence as your digital storefront

In the digital age, online presence is as critical as physical location. Having a strong website and active social media presence serves as your digital storefront. CapsuleCRM warns that a weak online presence means you are invisible in the vast digital marketplace[43]. Customers research products and services online before purchasing; if they cannot find you, they may choose a competitor.

Selecting the right location

When choosing a physical location, consider:

- **Demographics:** Ensure the local population matches your target market. Research income levels, age distribution, lifestyle preferences and foot traffic patterns.
- **Competition:** Too many competitors in a small area can saturate the market, while too few may indicate a lack of demand.
- **Costs:** Rent, utilities and taxes vary by neighborhood and city. A prime location may increase sales but also increase expenses. Balance visibility with affordability.
- **Zoning and regulations:** Local zoning laws may restrict certain types of businesses. Ensure your chosen site complies with regulations.

Building an effective website

Your website is often the first point of contact with customers. Essential elements include:

- **Clear value proposition:** Communicate what you offer and why visitors should care within seconds of landing on the page.
- **Responsive design:** Ensure your site looks good and functions well on desktops, tablets and smartphones.
- **Intuitive navigation:** Organize information logically and provide a clear path to important sections (products, pricing, contact).
- **Compelling content:** Provide informative descriptions, high-quality images or videos and calls-to-action. Use search-engine-optimized (SEO) keywords to improve visibility.

- **Fast load times:** Slow websites frustrate visitors and impact search rankings. Optimize images and minimize script load times.
- **Trust signals:** Include testimonials, reviews, security badges and clear return policies to build credibility.

Leveraging social media

Social media platforms allow you to interact with customers, build community and promote your brand. Choose platforms where your target audience spends time. Post regularly, respond to comments and messages promptly and provide value rather than constant sales pitches. User-generated content, such as customer photos and reviews, enhances authenticity and social proof. Run targeted ads to reach specific demographics and geographies.

Integrating online and offline channels

Deliver a seamless customer experience across physical and digital channels. Use strategies such as:

- **Click-and-collect:** Allow customers to order online and pick up in store. This drives foot traffic and convenience.
- **Omnichannel promotions:** Coordinate promotions across channels, ensuring consistent messaging.
- **Customer relationship management (CRM):** Use CRM systems to track interactions and personalize communication. Integrate in-store purchases with online profiles to gain a holistic view of customer behavior.

Evaluating location and presence regularly

Review your location's performance and digital analytics regularly. If foot traffic declines, consider relocating or renegotiating rent. Monitor website traffic sources, bounce rates and conversion rates. Use A/B testing to improve digital performance and adapt to changing consumer habits.

In the next chapter, we explore the necessity of adaptation, agility and innovation in a rapidly evolving business environment.

Chapter 12

Adaptation to Market Changes

The inevitability of change

Markets, technologies, customer preferences and regulatory environments change continually. Businesses that become complacent risk obsolescence. The U.S. Chamber of Commerce emphasizes that adaptability is essential to keeping up with our ever-changing cultural needs and economic climate[50]. Adjusting to market changes is not optional; it is critical for longevity.

Types of change

- **Technological change:** Innovations such as artificial intelligence, e-commerce and mobile technologies reshape industries. Firms that fail to adopt new technologies risk falling behind.
- **Consumer behavior:** Shifts in preferences—such as increased demand for sustainable products or digital convenience—create new opportunities and threats. For example, the rise of plant-based diets spurred new food companies while challenging traditional meat producers.
- **Economic cycles:** Inflation, interest rates, exchange rates and recession or expansion cycles impact purchasing power, financing costs and demand. High inflation in 2024 (3.5 %) made conditions tougher for new businesses[9].
- **Regulatory changes:** Laws governing taxation, labor, environmental protection and data privacy evolve.

Compliance costs and operational adjustments may be significant.

- **Societal trends:** Social movements, demographic shifts and cultural trends influence consumer expectations and reputational risks. Companies ignoring societal issues may face boycotts or reputational damage.

Building adaptability into your business

Cultivate a learning culture: Encourage employees to learn continuously, experiment and share insights. Provide training, attend conferences and invest in professional development.

Implement agile methodologies: Borrowing from software development, agile practices emphasize iterative development, cross-functional collaboration and responsiveness. Use sprints to test new ideas and gather feedback quickly.

Scenario planning: Explore multiple scenarios (best case, worst case, most likely) and develop contingency plans. Scenario planning forces you to consider how different variables could impact the business and to prepare responses.

Diversify offerings: Diversification reduces reliance on a single revenue stream. Offer complementary products or services that appeal to the same customers. For example, a restaurant might diversify with catering or meal kits.

Monitor key indicators: Track leading indicators such as changes in customer enquiries, supply-chain delays or competitor moves. Early warning signals allow timely adjustments.

Encourage innovation: Allocate resources to research and development. Reward employees who suggest improvements or propose new products. A dedicated innovation team or lab can explore emerging trends.

Responding to disruptions

When disruptions occur, such as a pandemic, natural disaster or supply-chain breakdown, rapid response is crucial. Steps include:

- **Activate your contingency plan:** Implement predefined actions to protect employees, stabilize operations and communicate with stakeholders.
- **Reassess demand:** Identify how customer needs change during the disruption. For example, during the COVID-19 pandemic, demand for take-out and delivery surged.
- **Adjust operations:** Modify hours, delivery methods or product lines to align with new conditions. Restaurants pivoted to contactless delivery; gyms offered online classes.
- **Communicate transparently:** Keep employees, customers and partners informed about changes and what you are doing to address challenges.
- **Seek support:** Leverage government assistance, financial relief programs and industry networks. Many governments offer grants and loans to help businesses survive crises.

Learning from failure and pivoting

Failure can be a catalyst for growth if you extract lessons and pivot strategically. Many successful companies pivoted from their original idea after initial setbacks. Slack started as a gaming company before pivoting to team communication; Netflix pivoted from DVD rentals to streaming. Key principles for pivoting include:

- **Recognize when the model is failing:** Look for signs such as declining sales, customer dissatisfaction or rising acquisition costs.
- **Identify alternative opportunities:** Use customer feedback, market research and data to identify new opportunities that align with your capabilities.
- **Develop a transition plan:** Outline how you will shift resources, change marketing and communicate with stakeholders.
- **Act decisively:** Pivoting requires commitment. Once you decide to change direction, allocate resources and align the organization around the new strategy.

Adaptability is a mindset and capability that ensures your business remains relevant and resilient. The following chapter focuses on scaling your business sustainably without overextending resources.

Chapter 13

Scaling and Sustainable Growth

The growth paradox

Growth is a double-edged sword. On one hand, expansion increases revenue, market share and economies of scale. On the other, growing too fast can overstrain resources, degrade customer experience and create cash-flow crises. FibreCU notes that companies that find early success sometimes overexpand, overwhelming their resources and reserves[18]. Georgia's SBDC warns that rapid growth can lead to a cash-flow crisis[51]. Sustainable scaling requires careful planning, systems and discipline.

Building scalable systems

Standardize processes: Document processes for operations, customer service, marketing and finance. Standardization allows tasks to be replicated consistently as you add team members.

Invest in technology: Use software to automate repetitive tasks and manage complexity. Customer relationship management (CRM) systems, enterprise resource planning (ERP) software and marketing automation tools increase efficiency and reduce reliance on manual processes.

Hire strategically: Hire staff ahead of demand, but not too early. Use fractional or temporary workers to handle surges until you can justify permanent hires. Ensure that new hires align with culture and values.

Monitor capacity: Understand the capacity of your systems and people. For example, a manufacturer must know its production limits to avoid bottlenecks when orders increase.

Align finances: Ensure that cash-flow and funding support growth. Do not invest in growth initiatives unless you have the capital to sustain them. Use financial models to assess how growth affects cash-flow, profitability and balance sheet health.

Product and market expansion

Market penetration: Increase market share by reaching new customers in your existing market. Use targeted marketing campaigns, partnerships or promotions.

Market development: Enter new geographic markets or new customer segments. Research cultural, regulatory and economic differences to adapt your offering.

Product development: Develop new products or services for your existing market. Use customer feedback to identify unmet needs and innovate accordingly.

Diversification: Expand into new products and markets simultaneously. Diversification spreads risk but requires careful analysis and adequate resources.

Maintaining quality during growth

Rapid growth can compromise quality if systems and training do not scale. To preserve quality:

- **Implement quality controls:** Use checklists, audits and key quality metrics to monitor performance.
- **Train employees:** Provide training programs to ensure new hires understand standards and processes.
- **Gather feedback:** Collect feedback from customers and frontline employees. Address issues quickly.
- **Stay customer-centric:** Keep customer satisfaction at the center of decision-making. Scale should not come at the expense of the customer experience.

Avoiding growth traps

- **Overextension:** Do not expand into new markets or product lines until your core business is stable and profitable.
- **Ignoring culture:** Rapid hiring can dilute culture. Maintain values and hire for fit.
- **Underestimating working capital:** Growth often requires purchasing more inventory, hiring more staff or extending credit to customers. Ensure you have sufficient working capital.
- **Neglecting infrastructure:** Failing to upgrade systems or facilities may lead to breakdowns during peak demand.

Exit considerations when scaling

Scaling sets the stage for a potential exit. Investors and acquirers look for businesses with proven growth trajectories, scalable systems and strong management teams. Keep detailed records, maintain strong governance and ensure intellectual property is protected. Consider how your decisions today, such as ownership structure, debt levels and partner agreements, could affect future exit options.

Scaling is an exciting phase that brings new challenges and opportunities. By planning carefully and focusing on sustainable growth, you can expand without jeopardizing your business. The next chapter addresses legal, regulatory and risk management issues; areas often overlooked until problems arise.

Chapter 14

Legal, Regulatory and Risk Management

The importance of compliance

Legal and regulatory compliance is not optional. Failure to adhere to laws and regulations can result in fines, lawsuits, license revocation or even closure. Many entrepreneurs focus on product development and marketing but neglect legal requirements until it is too late. A comprehensive understanding of applicable laws reduces risk and demonstrates professionalism.

Key legal considerations

Business structure: Choose the appropriate legal structure (sole proprietorship, partnership, corporation, limited liability company) based on liability, taxation and control considerations. Register your business and obtain necessary permits and licenses.

Contracts and agreements: Draft contracts for employees, suppliers, customers and partners. Clear contracts define expectations, responsibilities, payment terms and dispute resolution mechanisms. Use lawyers to review contracts to ensure enforceability and compliance with local laws.

Employment law: Understand laws related to hiring, compensation, workplace safety, anti-discrimination, harassment and termination. Provide employee handbooks and training to ensure compliance.

Intellectual property (IP): Protect your IP through trademarks, copyrights and patents. IP is a valuable asset that differentiates your business and can increase valuation.

Data privacy: If you collect customer data, comply with data protection laws like the General Data Protection Regulation (GDPR) or California Consumer Privacy Act (CCPA). Implement security measures to protect data and notify authorities of breaches as required.

Tax compliance: Understand federal, state and local tax obligations. Use accountants to ensure accurate filings and to take advantage of available deductions.

Risk management

Risk management involves identifying, assessing and mitigating risks that could threaten the business. Common risks include:

- **Operational risks:** Process failures, equipment breakdowns and supply-chain disruptions. Mitigate by implementing standard operating procedures, preventive maintenance and diversified suppliers.
- **Financial risks:** Cash-flow shortfalls, bad debt, interest rate fluctuations and currency risks. Mitigate through cash-flow management, credit checks on customers, hedging and insurance.
- **Legal risks:** Lawsuits, contract disputes and regulatory violations. Mitigate by using sound contracts, obtaining legal counsel and complying with laws.
- **Reputational risks:** Negative publicity, customer complaints and social media backlash. Mitigate by

providing high-quality products, excellent service and transparent communications.

- **Strategic risks:** Poor strategic decisions, market shifts or competitive threats. Mitigate through regular strategic reviews, market monitoring and scenario planning.

Insurance

Insurance transfers risk to an insurer in exchange for a premium. Types of insurance include:

- **General liability:** Covers bodily injury, property damage and personal injury claims.
- **Professional liability:** Protects against negligence claims related to professional services.
- **Property insurance:** Covers damage to buildings, equipment and inventory.
- **Workers' compensation:** Provides benefits to employees injured on the job.
- **Business interruption:** Compensates for lost income during events that halt operations (e.g., fire, natural disasters).

Work with a broker to identify the appropriate coverage for your industry and risk profile. Review policies regularly and adjust coverage as your business grows or changes.

Building a risk-aware culture

Incorporate risk management into everyday operations. Train employees to identify and report risks. Establish escalation procedures for potential crises. Conduct regular audits and stress tests to assess the effectiveness of controls. A risk-aware culture reduces surprises and fosters proactive management.

When to seek professional advice

Do not hesitate to consult legal, tax and insurance professionals. Their expertise helps you navigate complex regulations, avoid costly mistakes and ensure comprehensive coverage. Invest in professional relationships early to build trust and understanding.

Risk management and legal compliance are foundational elements that support growth and sustainability. The next chapter examines how external factors, beyond your control, can impact your business and what you can do to prepare.

Chapter 15

External Factors and Crisis Preparedness

Recognizing external threats

External factors are events or conditions outside the business's control that can affect operations. These include economic downturns, inflation, supply-chain disruptions, natural disasters, pandemics and geopolitical events. The 2024 inflation rate (3.5 %) added difficulty for new businesses[9], while the COVID-19 pandemic illustrated how a health crisis can shut down entire sectors. Understanding external threats allows businesses to prepare and respond effectively.

Economic and market forces

Economic cycles influence consumer spending, borrowing costs and investment. During recessions, consumers cut discretionary spending, which affects sectors like hospitality and retail. High interest rates increase borrowing costs, reducing investment. Conversely, economic expansion creates opportunities for growth. Monitor economic indicators (GDP growth, unemployment, inflation, consumer confidence) and adapt your strategies accordingly.

Supply-chain disruptions

Global supply chains are vulnerable to disruptions from natural disasters, geopolitical tensions and transportation issues. Companies reliant on a single supplier or region risk stockouts and production halts. Mitigate by diversifying suppliers, maintaining safety stock and monitoring supply-chain risks.

Health crises and natural disasters

Health crises such as pandemics and natural disasters such as hurricanes, floods and wildfires can disrupt operations and demand. During COVID-19, many businesses pivoted to online operations or implemented safety protocols. Have contingency plans for remote work, alternative distribution channels and emergency response. Purchase business interruption insurance to mitigate financial losses.

Political and regulatory changes

Changes in laws, tariffs or trade policies can impact costs, market access and compliance requirements. For example, increased tariffs on imported goods raise input costs, while new data privacy laws require investments in compliance. Monitor regulatory developments through industry associations and legal counsel. Engage in advocacy through trade groups to influence policies.

Crisis management planning

Develop a crisis plan: Outline steps for identifying, managing and communicating during a crisis. Include roles, responsibilities and escalation protocols.

Create communication templates: Prepare messages for employees, customers, suppliers and media. Effective communication maintains trust and prevents misinformation.

Establish contingency teams: Designate cross-functional teams to lead response efforts. Train them on crisis protocols and conduct drills.

Maintain emergency funds: Cash reserves are vital during crises. Ensure that you have accessible funds to cover essential expenses when revenue drops.

Review and update regularly: Update your crisis plan after drills or real events. Incorporate lessons learned and changing risks.

Building resilience

Resilience is the ability to withstand shocks and recover quickly. Build resilience by diversifying revenue streams, investing in technology that facilitates remote operations, developing strong relationships with suppliers and customers and fostering a culture that embraces change. Businesses that survived the pandemic often had flexible business models, digital capabilities and strong community connections.

External factors will continue to pose challenges. By anticipating and preparing for crises, entrepreneurs can mitigate impacts and even find opportunities in adversity. The final chapter addresses how to exit a business—an aspect of planning that many overlook until it is too late.

Chapter 16

Exiting the Business: Succession and Exit Planning

Why exit planning matters

Every business owner will eventually exit; whether through a sale, succession, merger or closure. Planning for that inevitable exit early maximizes value, ensures continuity for employees and customers and provides financial security for the owner. Exit planning is not about pessimism; it is about having a strategy for the endgame. To be clear, there is always an exit in the future, the question is: Will it be on your terms or someone else's?

Exit options

There are actually countless considerations of how to exit, this short list represents a few of the most common solutions, you may even use combinations of these as well as others. So don't get so fixated on how you intend to exit, so much as that an exit is inevitable and seek advice on what the best options for you may be.

To be clear, what sounds like a great idea today, may not be in the cards a few years from now, or there may be even better options. The key is in identifying what causes exit challenges and how to appropriately prepare to have as many options as possible when the time comes.

- **Sale to a third party:** Selling to another individual, company or private equity firm. Requires preparing the business for due diligence, ensuring financials are transparent and maximizing valuation.
- **Succession to family or employees:** Transferring ownership to a family member or key employee. Requires training successors, documenting processes and managing family dynamics. This process often takes 2 to 3 years, if you haven't adequately prepared throughout the life of the company.
- **Management buyout (MBO):** The management team buys the business, often financed through loans or investors.
- **Merger:** Combining with another company can create synergies and provide an exit for owners.
- **Liquidation:** Closing and selling assets. Typically yields the lowest return and is considered when other options are unviable. Unfortunately for most business owners, this happens is as much as 80% of all privately held organizations.

Preparing for an exit

Strengthen financial statements: Buyers and investors scrutinize financials. Use accurate accounting, eliminate discretionary expenses and demonstrate consistent profitability. Ensure that personal expenses are not commingled with business accounts. To provide yourself with the best odds of selling and the potential acquirer with the best insights to make such an important decision, it would be prudent to have at minimum of the last 2 years with very clean financials. Depending on the age of your business, or the growth trajectory, this may need to be more like 3 to 5 years. Most owners don't have this in place.

Diversify customer base: Overreliance on a few customers reduces valuation dramatically. Develop a broad customer base to show stable revenue streams.

Document systems and processes: Procedures that are well-documented make the business less dependent on the owner. This increases attractiveness to buyers and smooths transitions. Often owners only consider operations when we discuss documenting SOP (Standard Operating Procedures), however, this includes Sales and Marketing strategies with the data to support the ROI of said marketing and a proven track record of sales performances through a documented system and training protocol.

Protect intellectual property: Register trademarks, copyrights or patents. Ensure that licenses and contracts are transferable.

Address legal and tax issues: Work with lawyers and tax advisors to structure the sale or succession efficiently. Consider the tax implications of different exit strategies.

Communicate with stakeholders: Inform key employees and partners about your plans early. Transparent communication builds trust and reduces uncertainty.

Timing the exit

The timing of your exit influences the value you receive. Monitor market conditions, industry trends and personal goals. Selling during periods of strong performance and favorable economic conditions typically yields better outcomes. Avoid waiting until you are forced to sell due to burnout, health issues or financial stress, as distress sales often fetch lower prices. Also know that the value of an experienced broker or representative to help you navigate this process is a necessity. Whatever fee you pay to the right person, should provide you with a return of 5 to 10-fold.

Successor development

When passing the business to a family member or employee, they invest in their development. Provide training, mentorship and gradually increase their responsibilities. Clarify roles, expectations and ownership transfer mechanisms. Document governance structures to manage potential family conflicts.

Life after exit

Plan for your post-exit life. Consider whether you want to retire, pursue new ventures, consult or engage in philanthropy. Financial planning ensures that proceeds from the sale or succession support your desired lifestyle. Emotional preparation is also important; many entrepreneurs struggle with identity after leaving a business they built.

Common exit pitfalls

- **Procrastination:** Delaying exit planning reduces options and value. Start planning several years before your intended exit.

- **Ignoring taxes:** Failing to consider tax implications can erode proceeds. Consult tax professionals early.
- **Overvaluing the business:** Owners often overestimate their company's worth. Conduct valuations using professional appraisers or market comparables. Ensure that your expectations are grounded in reality before you are forced to face a rude awakening.
- **Neglecting team and customers:** Sudden exits without preparation can dramatically harm employee and customer relations. Involve stakeholders and ensure continuity plans.

Conclusion: leaving a legacy

Exiting a business is not an end but a transformation. With thoughtful planning, you can secure financial returns, ensure the company's continued success and create opportunities for future leaders. Whether you hand the business to a successor or sell it, your legacy lives on through the people you hired, the customers you served and the innovations you brought to the market.

Conclusion of Section 1

Entrepreneurship is a journey full of challenges and opportunities. Thus far in this book we have explored the many reasons businesses fail and suggested a few basic strategies to avoid those pitfalls. Understanding failure statistics allows you to appreciate the scale of the challenge, while analyzing the root causes; such as lack of market demand[16], cash-flow problems[3], poor planning[12], inadequate marketing[17], weak management[11], overexpansion[18] and external shocks[19], which should provide a roadmap for building resilient businesses.

By conducting thorough market research, crafting solid business plans, securing adequate financing, setting the right prices, investing in marketing, developing leadership and building strong teams, entrepreneurs can overcome many common obstacles. Additionally, staying attuned to competition, choosing the right location, maintaining a strong digital presence, adapting to change, scaling sustainably, managing legal and regulatory risks, preparing for external crises and planning exit strategies all contribute to long-term success.

Ultimately, success is not guaranteed, but failure is not inevitable. Armed with knowledge, determination and adaptability, entrepreneurs can transform ideas into thriving enterprises that withstand the tests of time and adversity. Let this insight serve as both a cautionary tale and an inspiration, guiding you as you start, grow, scale and eventually exit your business on your own terms.

Section II

The Solution Framework

Chapter 17

The 7 Core Competencies: Forged in the Field, Proven in the Fire

Most business frameworks are built in boardrooms.

Mine was built in combat boots, boxing gloves, retail storefronts, acquisition war rooms, and in the uncomfortable silence of writing seven-figure checks to fix my own mistakes.

The 7 Core Competencies were not invented.
They were discovered.

Discovered through pattern recognition across 30 years of leadership, 25 years in wireless while assisting in scaling two companies to well over $100 million, 15 businesses of my own, startups, acquisitions, exits (good and bad), including two powerful lessons that cost me millions, and more than 140 companies coached over the last six and a half years.

I didn't sit down one day and say, "Let me create a framework."
I kept asking one question:

Why do some (a select few) businesses scale and exit successfully… and others (the majority) collapse under their own weight?

The answer kept repeating itself.

The Early Foundations: Discipline, Adaptability, and Pattern Recognition

The Military: Structure Wins Wars

My time in the military taught me something simple and non-negotiable:

- Clarity of mission
- Chain of command
- Accountability
- Execution under pressure

There is no "kind of" clear objective in combat.
There is no "mostly" aligned team.

You either execute… or you don't.

That obsession with clarity and structure became the backbone of what would later become:

- **Leadership & Vision**
- **Operational Excellence**
- **People Management**

You can't scale chaos. You can only scale structure.

Professional Kickboxing: Synthesize or Lose

As a professional kickboxer, I studied five different fighting styles.

Five.

Not because it looked impressive.
Because each style had a blind spot from what I could see and not everyone of them was ideal for my body style or abilities.

I took what worked for me from each:

- The discipline of traditional martial arts, Tang Soo Do
- The aggression of Muay Thai
- The precision of Boxing
- The kicking of Taekwondo
- The fluidity of hybrid systems such as Jeet Kune Do.

Then I engineered my own championship style. That lesson never left me.

When I later evaluated business systems, coaching models, leadership philosophies, and growth strategies, I didn't adopt them blindly. I dissected them.

I asked:

- What works?
- What fails?
- Why?
- Under what conditions?
- At what stage of growth?

That same synthesis mindset ultimately shaped the 7 Core Competencies and the 8 Phases of Scale.

Nothing theoretical. Everything field-tested.

The 25-Year Laboratory: The Wireless Industry

For 25 years, I was the "Fix-It" guy.

Underperforming region? Send Eric.
Cultural breakdown? Send Eric.
Stalled revenue? Send Eric.
Post-acquisition integration? Send Eric.

Over and over again, I was dropped into businesses doing millions in revenue that had plateaued, fractured, or drifted.

And every time, I ran the same mental diagnostic:

1. Is leadership clear?
2. Are the numbers understood?
3. Are sales structured?
4. Are operations systemized?
5. Are people aligned?
6. Is customer experience consistent?

It didn't matter whether the company had 5 locations or 50. The breakdown was always in one or more of these areas.

I had the privilege of helping scale two organizations to well over $100 million annually.
Multiple acquisitions. Complex integration challenges. Cultural transformations.

And eventually, a successful exit in 2017 approaching nine figures. That exit changed everything for me.

Because here's what most people don't understand:

- Revenue growth does not guarantee enterprise value.
- You can build a $100 million revenue company that is unsellable, or at least only receive a fraction of the value, because you didn't build it right.

That realization sharpened the framework further.

15 Businesses: Humility Through Ownership

In addition to building a corporate career, I started or acquired 8 of my own 15 businesses while holding down a "day job".

Of the 15, some crossed $1 million annually.
One trucking company scaled to $6 million in under a year.

Some ventures thrived. Some nearly took me out. Twice, I learned lessons that cost me hundreds of thousands of dollars.

Those lessons were not market problems.

They were competency gaps:

- I overestimated operational capacity.
- I underestimated financial exposure.
- I trusted growth without systems.
- I expanded faster than infrastructure.

Pain is an exceptional teacher.

Ownership has a way of removing theoretical comfort. When it's your capital, your reputation, your liability, your family's future… clarity arrives quickly. That's when I began seeing something deeper.

Success wasn't random.
Failure wasn't random.

Both were patterned.

The Transition to Coaching: 140+ Businesses Later

When I exited the wireless industry and launched My Biz Coaches, I thought I would simply transfer experience.

Instead, I began running a six-year experiment.

Over 140 businesses.
Startups.
Plateaued companies.
Acquisition-minded founders.
Burned-out owners.
Fast-growth operators.

And the same themes kept emerging.

Not occasionally.

Repeatedly.

A founder would struggle with cash flow.
It traced back to financial discipline – Financial Acumen.

A company would plateau at $2M.
It traced back to Leadership & Vision misalignment.

A team implosion would occur.
It traced back to Leadership & Vision and People Management.

A business would grow fast but become chaotic.
It traced back to Operational Excellence.

A company would fail to sell.
It traced back to Transferability gaps due to inconsistent systems, poor financials, and no clear leadership transition plan.
Operational Excellence, Financial Acumen, and Leadership & Vision.

Over and over.

I began documenting patterns obsessively. Probably to the annoyance of anyone who has ever worked for me.

I have always been the person asking:

- Why do we do it that way?
- What is the system?
- What happens if volume doubles?
- What happens if we lose the owner?
- What breaks first?

Let's be honest. That curiosity has likely made me a less-than-ideal employee. But it made me a dangerous operator and fierce competitor. And eventually, it made the framework inevitable.

From Six to Seven: The Missing Variable

Originally, there were six Core Competencies.

1. Leadership & Vision
2. Financial Acumen
3. Sales & Marketing
4. Operational Excellence
5. People Management
6. Customer Service

For years, these six held up extremely well.

They were derived from decades of experience building businesses, scaling organizations, and studying what separated companies that grew from those that stalled. They reflected the operational reality that every successful organization must master leadership, money, people, operations, sales, and customer experience.

And for a time, those six were enough. However, things had changed. Markets began moving faster. Technology accelerated. Entire industry Titans had begun to crumble and become just a shell of who they once were, almost in front of our eyes. It was becoming so obvious, as this was not just a lack of relevance, but to complete implosion. I watched this playout all through my last 10 years in retail watching retail titan after retail titan fall: Montgomery Wards, Sears, Toys R Us, Blockbuster, Bed Bath & Beyond, and JC Penney, some of those names had been in business for over 100 years.

At the same time, what seemed suddenly, entire industries began evolving in half the time they used to. New Titans were rising from seemingly nowhere: Uber, Canva, Zoom, AirBnB, Shopify, Netflix, Nvidia, Stripe.

And then, artificial intelligence entered the equation…

What used to be a **20 to 30-year industry lifecycle** had begun shrinking to **10–15 years**. Now, with the rapid development of AI, automation, and digital platforms, entire business models are at risk of becoming outdated in three to five years.

Three to five years.

Let that sink in.

A business model that works today may still generate revenue next year… but within a few short years, the underlying structure that supports it may already be obsolete. And that realization forced me to confront something uncomfortable. I began seeing companies that were strong in **all six competencies**…

Yet they were still declining.

These businesses had capable leadership.
They understood their financials.
Their sales teams were competent.
Operations were disciplined.
They had good people and loyal customers.

And yet they were slowly losing relevance.

Why?

Because they resisted adaptation. They were running excellent businesses… built for yesterday's market. That is when it became clear something was missing. In the realization, I was reminded of a book I had read many years earlier titled "Built to Last" by Jim Collins and Jerry Porras. In the book they outlined a 6-year Standford study that identified a list of 18 companies that had lasted for decades and were recognized as "visionary companies". I remembered one of the concepts that were introduced as defining a company as visionary, was the idea of "preserve the core and stimulate progress".

The Core represented a company's purpose, mission, and core values. The leadership lesson was that the company's values should stay permanent, but the methods in achieving the goals should remain flexible. Too many companies were clinging to outdated strategies while casually abandoning the very values that should guide them. Meaning a "visionary company" would maintain a clear identity while constantly reinventing how they deliver value to the market, or more specifically, how they win.

That was it! The framework needed a seventh competency. Not a replacement for the fundamentals and I can't simply envelope it into Operational Excellence, as I had been doing in my mind. That didn't call enough attention to the impact. No, this needed its own Competency, as it would continue to have major impact on businesses into the foreseeable future.

This Competency would provide the capability that ensured the fundamentals could **evolve fast enough to remain relevant.** That missing variable became undeniable.

The Seventh Core Competency

Innovation & Technology

Or more precisely:

Resilience in Change.
Relevance Through Innovation.

This competency is not about chasing shiny objects. It is not about adopting technology for the sake of looking modern. It is about disciplined evolution.

The ability of a business leader to continually ask:

- How is our industry changing?
- How is technology reshaping customer expectations?
- Which parts of our business model will become obsolete?
- How can we leverage emerging tools before competitors do?

Innovation & Technology means developing the capacity to:

- Adapt strategy
- Reposition offers
- Leverage technology
- Reinvent operations
- Improve decision speed
- Shift business models when necessary

Without abandoning the fundamentals. Because the fundamentals still matter.

Leadership still matters.
Financial discipline still matters.
Sales still matter.
Operations still matter.
People still matter.
Customer experience still matters.

But in a world where industries evolve faster than ever before, **mastering those six alone is no longer enough.** Without the ability to innovate and adapt, even well-run businesses can slowly fade into irrelevance and even faster than ever before. This seventh competency closed the gap.

It explained why strong companies sometimes fail during disruption. It explained why new competitors suddenly appear and dominate markets. And it explained why certain organizations seem to thrive even in chaotic environments.

They are not simply well managed.

They are **adaptive**.

They evolve faster than their competitors.

And in today's economy, that may be the most important survival trait of all. Because the future will not belong to the biggest businesses. It will belong to the ones that learn, adapt, and innovate the fastest.

I'll simply end with this…

"The question is no longer whether innovation and technology will reshape your industry.
The only question is whether you will leverage them to scale your business… or wait until they scale your competitors instead."

The 8 Phases of Scale: Context Matters

One of the biggest mistakes in business education is generic advice. Telling a startup to behave like a $20M company is malpractice. Telling a $10M company to operate like a startup is equally destructive. That is why the Core Competencies must be applied within the 8 Phases of Scale to be completely effective.

Because:

- Early-phase businesses need focus.
- Mid-phase businesses need infrastructure.
- Growth-phase businesses need delegation.
- Exit-phase businesses need transferability.

Competency doesn't change. The **application does**. That distinction is everything.

Why This Matters

Only about 6% of businesses ever reach $1 million in annual revenue. Even fewer build true transferable enterprise value.

Most owners:

- Work too many hours.
- Own jobs, not businesses.
- Lack financial clarity.
- Cannot step away.
- Cannot sell.
- Cannot scale without breaking.

That is not a motivation problem. It is a competency alignment problem.

The mission of My Biz Coaches is simple and yet quite ambitious:

Empower 1,000 businesses to achieve the Entrepreneur's Dream of building a multi-million-dollar, profitable, transferable business: Without sacrificing their entire life in the process.

This is not motivational speaking. This is structural engineering.

The Framework Was Not Created. It Emerged.

From:

- Military precision
- Championship-level synthesis
- Corporate scale
- Acquisition integration
- Near nine-figure exit
- Entrepreneurial scars
- Million-dollar mistakes
- 140+ business case studies
- Thousands of hours of pattern recognition

The 7 Core Competencies and 8 Phases of Scale are not theory. They are distilled repetition.

They are what remain after ego, optimism, and luck are removed.

The Commercial Aircraft Model - Visual Analogy

As I began to put this together, I was sharing with a peer who is an entrepreneur and a pilot and as I was describing the components of my framework, he offered this as a visual that I could use to share the concept.

- The 7 Core Competencies = The Flight Systems
- The 8 Phases of Scale = The Altitude Levels
- Leadership = Pilot
- Financial Acumen = Fuel System
- Sales & Marketing = Thrust
- Operations = Aerodynamics
- People Management = Crew
- Customer Focus = Navigation
- Innovation & Technology = Turbulence Management

He said that most everyone understands this truth: A plane doesn't crash because one thing goes wrong, it crashes because multiple systems fail at once.

That's similar in business.

- You can't run out of fuel and rely on good branding.
- Have thrust without direction.
- You must maneuver accordingly through turbulence.

The early stages of business are like the takeoff. Mid-stages are similar to the altitude climb. Maturity is like reaching cruising altitude, and Exiting a business is like landing a plane.

Here's the kicker, most entrepreneurs are:

- Flying without instruments.
- Flying Solo without training.
- They overcorrect when flying through turbulence because they are unaware or unfamiliar.

As a Coach you are teaching them to:

- Install the right systems to help them fly.
- Read the dashboard so they can make the appropriate adjustments.
- And you are showing them how to and how important it is to build redundancies in case things go wrong.

As he walked me through this, I was quite intrigued by how much similarity there seemed to be, however, I began to realize at that point, the framework I had developed wasn't so unique as much as I had never seen anyone apply it to businesses before.

In the chapters ahead

We will break each competency down. Not as philosophy. But as executable architecture. Because scaling is not mysterious. It is measurable.

And once you see the pattern… you can't unsee it.

Chapter 18

The Bedrock of the 7 Core Competencies - Leadership & Vision: The Growth Ceiling

Why Leadership & Vision is the Foundation of the 7 Core Competencies

Let's begin with a hard truth.

Most businesses don't fail because the owner lacked passion. They fail because the owner lacked integration.

After more than 30 years in business, assisting in scaling two companies past $100 million in annual revenue, starting or acquiring 15 businesses of my own, successfully participating in an exit in 2017, and working with over 140 clients in the last 6 years, I have seen this pattern repeatedly.

The problem is not effort. The problem is fragmentation.

Entrepreneurs are often strong in two, maybe three areas (sometimes it's just one). A select few are strong in four areas. Now, I didn't say aware, you can be aware of the importance, but that doesn't solve the gap. Long-term success demands mastery, or at minimum, strategic coverage (through key employees) across all seven Core Competencies:

1. Leadership & Vision
2. Financial Acumen
3. Sales & Marketing
4. Operational Excellence

5. Human Capital Management
6. Customer Focus (Client Fulfillment)
7. Innovation & Technology

These are not motivational concepts. They are structural requirements.

You can hire for them.
You can partner for them.
You can outsource them.

But you cannot ignore them.

And at the center of all seven sits the first and most critical competency:

Leadership & Vision.

It is not just the first competency. It is the bedrock.

Why Leadership Comes First

You do not build a scalable enterprise on tactics. You build it on direction.

Leadership answers the fundamental questions:

- Where are we going?
- Why are we going there?
- What does success look like?
- Who must we become to achieve it?

Without clear vision, the other six competencies operate independently. With strong leadership, they integrate into a cohesive system. A business without leadership clarity is like a high-performance engine with no steering wheel. It may move fast. It may generate revenue. But it will eventually crash.

The Business Will Never Outgrow the Leader

One principle has proven true across every company I've built or scaled and every business I have worked in, worked with, or studied:

The business will only grow to the level of the leader's maturity.

If the leader lacks discipline, the company lacks discipline. If the leader avoids difficult decisions, the organization becomes complacent. If the leader lacks long-term vision, the company plateaus.

You can have world-class marketing. You can have talented employees. You can have healthy margins. But if leadership is weak, inconsistent, or reactive, growth stalls.

Leadership is the ceiling.

Vision Aligns the Other Competencies

Every other competency depends on leadership clarity.

Financial Acumen

Financial data is neutral. Leadership determines interpretation. A P&L statement does not tell you whether to reinvest, expand, acquire, or conserve cash. The leader does. Financial strategy without vision becomes defensive bookkeeping. Financial strategy with vision becomes intentional capital deployment.

Sales & Marketing

You can grow revenue in ways that destroy enterprise value.

Chasing every customer.
Discounting to win.
Scaling unprofitable products.

Leadership determines positioning. Vision ensures you attract the right clients, protect margin integrity, and build brand equity, not just revenue.

Operational Excellence

Systems do not create discipline. Leadership does.

You can install project management software. You can implement KPIs. You can document SOPs. But unless leadership demands accountability and models operational rigor, execution deteriorates. Operational Excellence is culture operationalized.

Culture starts at the top.

Human Capital Management

Culture cannot be outsourced. It is modeled.

Leadership determines:

- What behaviors are rewarded
- What standards are enforced
- What accountability looks like
- How conflict is handled

Human Capital Management is simply leadership multiplied through others. If you struggle to delegate, the company bottlenecks. If you refuse to develop leaders, growth stalls. People scale businesses. Leaders develop people.

Customer Focus

Customer-centric companies are not accidental.

Leadership decides whether feedback is embraced or ignored. Leadership determines whether retention matters more than ego. Leadership chooses whether service is transactional or transformational.

Customer fulfillment reflects executive priorities.

Innovation & Technology

Markets change.
Technology evolves.
Competitors adapt.
Economic conditions shift.

Resilience is not a marketing tactic. It is a leadership posture. When pressure increases, leaders either panic or pivot.

Businesses that endure are led by individuals who embrace adaptation without abandoning vision.

Leadership Evolves at Every Phase of Scale

From Micro Business (Creator Phase) to Enterprise Scale (Investor Phase , the role of the leader must evolve.

In the early stages, you work in the business.
As you scale, you must learn to work on the business.

Eventually, you lead those who lead the business.

If you do not evolve, the company plateaus.

What got you to $250,000 will not get you to $1 million.
What got you to $1 million will not get you to $10 million.

Leadership maturity must expand in proportion to business growth.

Why This Matters to the Million-Dollar Dream

At My Biz Coaches, our mission is clear:

To empower 1,000 businesses to reach $1 million in annual revenue; profitably, without sacrificing everything else in life.

Only about 6% of businesses ever achieve the $1 million milestone – The sacrifice everything part is still too subjective to measure. Ask one of the 2 plus million business owners who have reached that milestone what they had to give up getting there. I am certain that it will make for some interesting stories.

To be clear, the 94% that didn't achieve the $1 million milestone, it wasn't because they lacked opportunity. It was likely because they lacked integration across the Core Competencies. Most owners are strong operators. Some are strong salespeople. A few are financially disciplined. But fewer still are those things AND are intentional leaders.

And without leadership, the system collapses.

Enterprise Value Is a Leadership Outcome

Nearly 80% of businesses listed for sale will never sell.

They generate revenue. They may even generate profit, even strong profits.

But they lack:

- Transferable systems
- Leadership depth
- Documented processes
- Cultural continuity
- Strategic positioning

All of those deficiencies trace back to leadership decisions made years earlier.

Exit value is not created at the point of sale.
It is created through disciplined leadership over time.

The Seven Competencies: An Integrated Framework

The 7 Core Competencies are not independent disciplines.

They are interdependent forces:

- Leadership defines direction.
- Financial Acumen protects and deploys capital.
- Sales & Marketing drive revenue.
- Operational Excellence ensures scalability.
- Human Capital Management multiplies capacity.
- Customer Focus drives retention and reputation.
- Innovation sustains relevance.

If even one is neglected, performance suffers. If multiple are neglected, failure accelerates.

Leadership is what aligns them.

The Responsibility of the CEO

Whether you are running a side hustle or leading a $25 million organization, the responsibility remains the same:

You must own leadership.

You may not personally execute every competency. But you must ensure each competency is covered; by hiring, partnering, or outsourcing.

You cannot delegate vision.
You cannot outsource accountability.
You cannot abdicate culture.

Leadership is not optional. It is foundational.

Final Thought

In the chapters ahead, we will explore balance of the 7 Core Competencies in detail; how they function, how they integrate, and how they must evolve through the 8 Phases of Scale.

But understand this clearly from the beginning:

Leadership & Vision is not just the first competency. It is the structural integrity of the entire framework. If it is strong, the rest can be built. If it is weak, nothing else will hold. And if your goal is to build a business that scales, sustains, and eventually sells on your terms, then leadership is where we begin.

Chapter 19

Financial Acumen: The Control System

The Superpower Most Entrepreneurs Ignore

There's a reason I put Financial Acumen second in the 7 Core Competencies.

Not because it's secondary. Because without it, the rest of your business becomes guesswork.

And I've learned, you don't build businesses on guesswork.

Where It Started: Northern Arizona University

My relationship with numbers didn't begin in a boardroom. It actually began in high school and extended through college.

Senior year of high school, while most students were trying to survive calculus, I took Accounting as my math credit. Not because I had some grand vision of becoming a CFO. I saw it as practical. Useful. Something that translated to real life.

And I loved it.

Accounting was exact. Balanced. Clean. There was a right answer and a wrong answer. Debits and credits either reconciled… or they didn't. No gray area. No fluff.

My teacher noticed it came easy to me. So instead of letting me coast, he challenged me. He had me tutor a peer through the class. That moment mattered more than I am sure either of us realized. Because when you can teach something, you truly understand it. I didn't just learn accounting. I internalized the logic behind it.

Years later, while attending Northern Arizona University as an Accounting major. I was on track. Good grades. Internship lined up. The traditional path toward CPA status was wide open. Then I had an honest moment with myself.

After my internship, actually during the internship, I realized something uncomfortable:

I didn't want to be an accountant!

I respected the discipline. I appreciated the structure. But I didn't see myself living inside spreadsheets for the rest of my life. So, I did what most displaced Accounting Major would do, I pivoted to Finance.

And that pivot changed everything.

Accounting Taught Me the Language

Finance Taught Me the Game

Accounting is the language of business. Finance is strategy. Accounting tells you what happened. Finance tells you what to do next.

Because of that early foundation, I could read financial statements the way some people read novels. Income statements. Balance sheets. Cash flow statements. They weren't intimidating. They were signals.

And here's what I started noticing over 30+ years in business:

Most entrepreneurs are functionally illiterate in the language of their own business. Not because they're unintelligent. Because they never learned how to read the scoreboard.

The Most Neglected Competency in Small Business

In the research on business failure, cash flow problems show up again and again as the leading cause of collapse. But let's be honest.

Cash flow isn't the root problem. It's the symptom.

The real issue is lack of financial acumen:

- Owners don't understand margins.
- They confuse revenue with profit.
- They scale sales without understanding cost structures.
- They wait until they "need money" to try to get approved for it.

And by then? It's too late. Or too expensive.

Over the past six years, working with more than 140 business owners, I've seen a consistent pattern:

Most entrepreneurs bring 2–4 of the core competencies into their business. Very few bring Financial Acumen with them. Which makes this the highest-leverage area for growth.

What Financial Acumen Really Means

This isn't about becoming a controller, CPA, or a CFO. It's about control.

Financial Acumen at its core means:

1. **You understand your numbers.**
2. **You make decisions based on data, not emotion.**
3. **You forecast before you feel pressure.**
4. **You treat cash flow like oxygen.**

Let's break this down in practical terms.

1. Cash Flow Management

Revenue does not equal health. I've seen $3M companies suffocating because they couldn't manage working capital. I've seen $750K companies thriving because they understood timing, receivables, and margin discipline.

If you don't know:

- Your monthly burn rate
- Your gross margin
- Your break-even point
- Your cash runway

You are flying blind. And blind pilots…Well, let's just say that doesn't end so well.

2. Financial Reporting Fluency

You should be able to read:

- An Income Statement
- A Balance Sheet
- And a Cash Flow Statement

Without waiting for your accountant to "interpret" it for you. In the Leader and Architect phases, this becomes non-negotiable. When you move from Operator Phase ($250K+) to Leader Phase ($500K) and beyond, financial review isn't quarterly. It's habitual. Often weekly. Sometimes daily.

Financial dashboards become strategic weapons.

3. Business Credit and Capital Strategy

Here's a hard truth:

If you try to get money when you need it, if you can even get it, you'll pay more for it and you'll jump through ridiculous hoops to get it. In the Creator and Hustler phases, building business credit before you need it is strategic positioning.

Credit cards. Lines of credit. Banking relationships.

You establish them in strength. Not in desperation. Because capital is fuel. And scaling requires fuel.

4. KPI Discipline

Financial Acumen is not about "checking the books."

It's about tracking the drivers:

- Cost per Acquisition (CPA)
- Customer Lifetime Value (LTV)
- Gross Margin %
- Net Profit %
- Return on Assets (ROA)
- Return on Investment (ROI)

When you scale to the Architect Phase ($1M to $3M), financial strategy replaces survival math .

Now we're talking:

- EBITDA
- Valuation multiples
- Capital deployment
- Acquisition modeling

Different level. Different game.

The Hidden Advantage

Here's what that accounting background gave me:

Pattern recognition.

Over time, I could walk into a business and within 15 minutes see the financial story behind the culture, the stress, and the bottlenecks.

Rachel Whitenhafer, a young marketing agency owner, once articulated something about me that clicked:

I have an unusual ability to recognize patterns across businesses.

That didn't come from charisma. It came from understanding numbers. Numbers don't lie. People do. Hope does. Emotion does.

But numbers? They're brutally honest. Sometimes, more than we would like, particularly as entrepreneurs. But, only when we know how to read them correctly.

Why This Competency Is So Dangerous to Ignore

You can survive weak marketing for a season. You can compensate for mediocre operations. You can even outwork leadership deficiencies for a while.

But weak Financial Acumen?

That kills companies.

Quietly.

Slowly.

Predictably.

And then owners say:

"We just ran out of money."

No.
You ran out of visibility.

Financial Acumen Across the Phases of Scale

Here's what this competency looks like across the journey:

Creator Phase ($0–$100K)

- Simple tracking system
- Basic accounting software
- Cash discipline
- No commingling of personal and business finances

You don't need complexity. You need clarity.

Hustler Phase ($100K–$250K)

- Hire a bookkeeper
- Work with a tax professional
- Begin business credit development
- Establish KPIs

This is where owners either mature… or stall.

Operator Phase ($250K–$500K)

- Daily KPI awareness
- Multiple banking relationships
- Margin discipline
- Lean operational mindset

Cash flow is king here.

Leader and Architect Phases ($500K–$3M)

- Fractional CFO engagement
- Investment decisions modeled, not guessed
- Strategic capital deployment
- Profit margin optimization (15–20% target at $1M)

Now you're building enterprise value.

Optimizer and Executive Phases ($3M - $25M)

- EBITDA focus
- Valuation multiples
- Acquisition analysis
- Enterprise value planning

Now you're not just running a business. You're building a valuable asset.

Investor Phase ($25M+)

- Capital allocation
- Mergers and Acquisitions
- Exit Strategy Planning

At this point, you are determining how to get your value out of the business.

The CEO Reality Check

If you are the Founder and you cannot:

- Explain your gross margin
- Forecast your cash position 90 days out
- Define your top 5 financial KPIs
- Articulate your break-even point

You are the bottleneck.

And that's not an insult. It's an invitation. Because Financial Acumen is learnable.

I didn't become financially disciplined because I was born that way. I was trained. Challenged. Refined. Tested in the real world across 15 businesses and executive roles in companies exceeding $100M in revenue.

This competency became my superpower. And it can become yours.

The Million-Dollar Filter

At My Biz Coaches, our mission is clear:

Help 1,000 businesses profitably achieve $1M in revenue. Only about 6% of businesses ever reach that milestone . You don't get there through hustle alone.

You get there through:

- Margin discipline
- KPI mastery
- Capital strategy
- Cash flow control

Financial Acumen is not optional at that level. It's mandatory.

Final Thought

Accounting showed me the structure. Finance showed me the strategy. Entrepreneurship showed me the stakes.

If Leadership is the engine, Financial Acumen is the fuel gauge.

Ignore it… and eventually you stall.

Master it… and you scale with confidence.

In the next chapter, we turn to Competency 3: Sales & Marketing; the revenue engine that feeds the numbers we just discussed. Because once you understand your financial scoreboard…Now it's time to move it.

Chapter 20

Sales & Marketing: The Growth Engine

Revenue is not an accident. It is engineered.

Let me be direct.

If you cannot sell, you do not have a business. If you cannot market, you will not have one for long.

I have spent over **30 years in sales** across retail, B2B wireless, big-box environments, insurance, high-ticket real estate investing programs, franchise sales, and just about every variation in between. I and the teams I have led have generated **over $1.3 billion in sales** throughout my career.

That number is not ego. It is evidence.

It represents thousands of conversations, thousands of objections, thousands of closing moments, and thousands of lessons in human psychology.

And here is what most entrepreneurs get wrong:

They treat Sales and Marketing like accessories. They are not accessories. They are oxygen.

Sales Is a Skill. Not a Personality Trait.

I've sold in:

- Commission-only environments
- Competitive big-box retail floors
- Enterprise B2B wireless contracts
- Insurance tables
- High-ticket investment programs
- Franchise development deals

Different products. Different buyers. Different price points. The fundamentals never changed.

Sales is:

- Listening before pitching
- Understanding pain before presenting solutions
- Communicating value before talking price
- Creating urgency without pressure
- Following up like a professional, not like a pest
- And, continuing to work to develop this craft, you must continue to stay sharp and train.

Many business owners are either:

- Afraid to sell
- Embarrassed to sell
- Or completely untrained in how to sell

And then they wonder why revenue stalls.

If you are the owner and cannot clearly and confidently sell your product or service, you have a structural weakness in your business model. That weakness compounds as you scale.

You can hire salespeople. But if you do not understand sales, you cannot train them, lead them, or hold them accountable.

That is a dangerous place to operate.

Marketing: The Discipline I Had to Humble Myself to Learn

Here is the truth.

For years, I dominated in traditional sales environments. Face-to-face. Territory management. Relationship selling. Team development.

Digital marketing?

Foreign language at that time in early 2019. So, when I launched My Biz Coaches, I made a decision.

Instead of pretending I understood digital marketing, I traded services with a marketing agency for my second client engagement. I coached them in business performance. They allowed me inside their machine.

- Campaign strategy.
- Funnels.
- SEO.
- Paid traffic.
- Brand positioning.

- Conversion tracking.
- Lead nurturing sequences.
- Retargeting.

I invested **tens of thousands of dollars** into understanding branding, messaging, funnels, and performance marketing. I did not outsource and hope it worked. I learned it and ensured it worked. I'll acknowledge Alex Hormozi on this one, I saw an interview where he discussed how he would learn new skills. One of the discussions turned to using vendors to uplevel skills for himself or his team. He mentioned he would invest in someone to provide insight and guidance, but he would pay extra to have them train him so he would gain the skill, or at least the insight into the skill, so he could then bring it in house.

That stuck with me.

Because here's the reality:

You cannot scale what you do not understand.

Four years later?

We launched our own marketing agency.

Why?

Because I saw too many business owners getting burned by:

- Agencies that could run ads but not drive profit
- Marketers who did not understand operations
- Branding experts who never sold anything in their life

- And Agencies who got results but because the client couldn't convert, the Agency got the bad rap for poor sales.

Marketing without operational understanding is expensive noise. Sales without marketing support is exhausting. When aligned correctly? It becomes the business growth engine.

The Sales & Marketing Competency Inside the 7 Core Competency Framework

Inside our 7 Core Competencies model , Sales & Marketing is not just "run ads and close deals."

It includes:

- A documented and repeatable sales process
- Clear brand positioning
- Defined target audience alignment
- CRM and lifecycle management
- Integrated organic + paid marketing
- Conversion tracking and performance metrics

And here is what I discovered working with over 140 clients:

Most entrepreneurs bring **1 to 3 competencies** naturally. Very few bring Sales AND Marketing mastery together.

They are often:

- Great at operations but weak at lead generation
- Great at marketing but poor at closing (Sales)
- Strong closers but no scalable pipeline
- Running ads but not tracking cost per acquisition
- Posting on social media with no strategy

It creates chaos disguised as activity. Revenue requires structure.

What $1.3 Billion in Sales Taught Me

Across three decades, here are the hard truths:

1. Marketing makes sales easier.
2. Sales converts what marketing creates.
3. Without metrics, both become emotional.
4. Without process, both become inconsistent.
5. Without leadership, both collapse under scale.

I have seen companies cross $100M in annual revenue because they aligned these disciplines correctly. I have also seen companies implode at $750K because they thought "more hustle" was the solution. Hustle without structure burns out founders. Structure with discipline builds enterprise value.

From Founder & CEO to Growth Architect

As Founder & CEO of My Biz Coaches, I bring:

- 30+ years in sales, operations, finance, and leadership
- Experience helping two companies exceed $100M annually
- Participated in a successful exit in 2017
- 15 businesses started or acquired
- A trucking company scaled to $6M in under a year
- Systems built around the 7 Core Competencies

Our mission is simple:

To help **1,000 business owners** achieve the Entrepreneur's Dream;
profitably reaching $1M in annual revenue (a feat only about 6% of businesses achieve), without sacrificing everything else in their life.

Sales & Marketing is one of the most misunderstood levers on that journey.

It is not about viral posts.
It is not about slick branding.
It is not about motivational closing scripts.

It is about:

- Message clarity
- Target precision
- Consistent activity
- Measured conversion
- Relentless refinement

Revenue is predictable when you treat it like a system.

Final Coaching Truth

If your revenue is inconsistent, the issue is not the economy.

It is not your competitors.
It is not the algorithm.

It is a gap in one of the following:

- Lead generation
- Conversion process
- Offer positioning
- Follow-up discipline
- Or tracking performance

Sales and Marketing are not optional competencies.

They are non-negotiable.

Master them. Or build a team that does.

Chapter 21

Operational Excellence: The Duplication Machine

The Engine That Makes Scale Possible

Let me be direct.

All the sales and marketing in the world will not save a business that cannot execute effectively.

You can generate leads.
You can close deals.
You can drive record-breaking revenue months.

But if your operations cannot support what you sell, your growth will implode under its own weight. Operational Excellence is not glamorous. It does not get applause at conferences. It does not trend on social media. But it is the difference between **momentum and mayhem**.

Sales Creates Opportunity. Operations Determines Capacity.

Throughout my career in the wireless industry, I was known primarily as a sales driver. I built teams. I grew regions. I fixed underperforming markets. I helped scale two companies beyond $100 million.

But at multiple points in my career, I had to step directly into operations. Because growth exposes every crack.

As a Regional GM, operations were not a theoretical concept. It was daily execution:

- Identifying retail sites
- Negotiating and overseeing build-outs
- Hiring and staffing stores
- Designing training programs
- Scheduling teams
- Managing inventory flow
- Tracking sales and performance
- Ensuring commissions were accurate
- Reconciling cash and accounts
- Monitoring compliance

Every single lever mattered.

You cannot scale retail without operational discipline. If inventory is off, sales stop. If commissions are inaccurate, morale collapses. If scheduling is inefficient, labor costs explode. If cash controls are weak, profits evaporate.

Growth magnifies operational flaws.

And here's what most business owners miss:

Revenue hides operational inefficiencies… until it doesn't.

The Cost of Inefficiency

Operational inefficiencies do not always scream. They whisper.

- A delayed onboarding process that slows productivity by two weeks.
- A broken inventory system that creates unnecessary backorders.
- A poorly designed commission structure that drives the wrong behaviors.
- A scheduling system that overpays for idle time.
- A CRM that sales ignores because it's clunky.

Individually, these seem small. Collectively, they stall scale.

I've watched businesses push harder on sales when the real constraint was operational. That is like stepping on the gas when the transmission is failing. You feel movement… until you hear the grinding.

As leaders, we must understand this principle:

Sales accelerates. Operations stabilizes.

Without stabilization, acceleration becomes chaos.

Pattern Recognition: The Operator's Superpower

One of the greatest advantages I developed over the years was pattern recognition.

When you oversee dozens, then hundreds of locations, patterns reveal themselves quickly:

- Stores that miss inventory audits also miss sales targets.

- Locations with high employee turnover show predictable performance decline within 90 days.
- Markets with inconsistent training produce inconsistent revenue.
- Regions that lack clean reporting lose margin quietly.

Operational problems are rarely isolated incidents. They are systemic. If you train yourself to look for patterns instead of events, you can identify breakdowns before they cost you millions.

Operational leaders must constantly ask:

- Where are delays happening?
- Where are bottlenecks forming?
- Where are errors recurring?
- Where are people compensating for broken systems?

When humans compensate for bad systems long enough, they burn out. When systems support humans effectively, they scale.

The Sales vs. Operations Tension

I spent years researching and analyzing the relationship between sales activity and operational performance.

Here is what I found:

1. Sales teams push for speed.
2. Operations demand structure.
3. When either side dominates, performance suffers.

If sales outruns operations:

- Customer experience declines.
- Errors increase.
- Refunds rise.
- Reputation erodes.

If operations overcontrols sales:

- Innovation slows.
- Agility dies.
- Opportunities are missed.

Operational Excellence is not about bureaucracy. It is about **optimized systems that support growth without suffocating it.**

The goal is simple:

Build systems that allow sales to thrive without breaking the machine.

Scaling Requires Systems, Not Heroics

In early-stage businesses, founders carry the load personally. They close the deals. They solve the problems. They fix the mistakes. But heroics do not scale.

Operational Excellence requires:

- Clear process documentation

- Defined roles and responsibilities
- Performance tracking
- Financial accountability
- Workflow optimization
- Measurable standards

When I stepped into struggling regions, I rarely found lazy people. I found unclear systems. People inherently want to win. Most are operating inside broken structures. Fix the structure. Performance improves.

The Hidden Stall Points in Scaling

As businesses move through the Phases of Scale, operational breakdowns appear in predictable ways:

Startup Phase (Creator & Hustler)

- No defined processes
- Everything lives in the owner's head
- Reactive execution

Growth Phase (Operator & Leader)

- Processes exist but are often undocumented
- Teams duplicate work
- Inconsistent delivery

Expansion Phase (Architect)

- Systems strain under volume
- Communication breaks down
- Reporting lags behind reality

Scale Phase (Optimizer)

- Legacy systems block innovation
- Complexity increases overhead
- Efficiency determines margin

At each phase, operational maturity must increase.

If it does not, growth stalls.

Efficiency is a Competitive Advantage

In retail operations, small efficiencies compound dramatically.

- Faster onboarding increases revenue ramp.
- Cleaner inventory systems reduce shrinkage.
- Accurate reporting improves forecasting.
- Structured scheduling protects margin.
- Clear training systems increase productivity.

I learned to view operations through one lens:

Where are we leaking time, money, or momentum?

Because leaks compound just as powerfully as efficiencies. Businesses do not fail because they lack effort. They fail because they lack systems that convert effort into scalable output.

Operational Excellence as a Strategic Discipline

Operational Excellence is not administrative. It is strategic.

It determines:

- Capacity for growth
- Cost structure
- Customer experience
- Employee retention
- Speed to market
- Profitability

If Leadership & Vision defines direction, and Sales & Marketing drives demand, then Operations determines whether the business can fulfill its promise.

And fulfillment is where reputation is built.

The Standard You Must Adopt

As a CEO, you must ask yourself:

- Are our systems scalable or fragile?
- Are we measuring what matters?
- Are inefficiencies visible or hidden?

- Do we rely on people's memories or documented processes?
- Are delays predictable or constant surprises?

Operational Excellence is not about perfection. It is about discipline. It is about designing systems intentionally rather than inheriting them accidentally.

When sales and operations are aligned, the business gains:

- Predictable revenue
- Stable margins
- Consistent customer experience
- Reduced stress
- Increased valuation

And valuation is where all roads eventually lead.

Operational Excellence is the engine.

Without it, growth becomes friction.

With it, scale becomes inevitable.

Chapter 22

People Management: The Multiplier Effect

IQ. EQ. SQ. If you're missing one, you're leading on one leg.

You can have vision.
You can understand your numbers.
You can build world-class systems.

But if you cannot lead people effectively, your business will stall. Period. People Management is not a "soft skill." It is a revenue lever. And it is one of the seven core competencies required to scale effectively .

People Are the Energy of the Business ⚡

If:

- Finances are the scorecard,
- Operations are the structure,

Then people are the energy that makes everything move.

No energy. No growth.

Over my 30+ year career, I have:

- Conducted or been involved in approximately 10,000 interviews
- Employed thousands
- Managed hundreds at a time
- Led teams that ranked #1 for multiple consecutive years

And here's what most people miss…

Those top-ranked sales teams did not win because we obsessed over sales techniques. We won because we developed leaders.

IQ, EQ, SQ – The Leadership Trinity

To lead at scale, you must develop:

1 IQ – Intelligence Quotient

Strategic thinking. Decision-making. Problem-solving.
You must understand the business model and think ahead.

2 EQ – Emotional Quotient

Self-awareness. Self-regulation. Empathy.
If you can't manage your emotions, you cannot manage a team.

3 SQ – Social Quotient

Influence. Communication. Cultural awareness.
Leadership is relational. If people don't trust you, they won't follow you.

Some individuals may have natural tendencies that make leading easier. But no one is "born a leader."

Leadership is forged.
Through experience.
Through feedback.
Through coaching.
Through failure.

Right People. Right Seats.

You've heard it before:

If you want to go fast, go alone. If you want to go far, go with a team. Scaling requires both direction and depth.

Your job as a leader is to:

- Identify strengths
- Align skills with roles
- Challenge people to elevate
- Delegate with clarity
- Hold others accountable

Wrong people in the wrong seats will sabotage scale faster than bad marketing ever will.

And here's a hard truth most founders avoid:

An "A" player will not work long-term for a "B" or "C" leader. If your leadership stagnates, top talent leaves. And what remains are "yes" people. "Yes" people do not challenge. They do not innovate. They do not stretch the organization.

They maintain mediocrity. And mediocrity compounds quietly over time.

Why Businesses Fail to Scale

One of the primary reasons businesses plateau between $500K and $1M is not marketing. It's not even capital. It's leadership capacity. As outlined across the phases of scale , every new revenue level requires a new version of the leader.

At:

- $100K → You must learn delegation.
- $500K → You must lead managers.
- $1M+ → You must lead leaders.
- $3M+ → You manage those who manage those who manage.

That is an entirely different skill set.

If you don't evolve, the business cannot.

Good. Let's tighten the screws a bit.

Because this is where most leaders lose control of their culture without even realizing it.

What Happens When Leadership Avoids Accountability

When leadership does **not** hold people accountable, three very predictable things happen.

And none of them are good.

1️⃣ The Best People Leave

Your top performers notice everything.

They see:

- Deadlines missed with no consequence
- Low standards tolerated
- Mediocre effort rewarded equally

High performers thrive in environments where excellence is the standard. When they are forced to carry underperformers, they don't complain loudly.

They disengage quietly. And then they leave.

"A" players want to be led by strong leaders and surrounded by other "A" players. When leadership is weak, they interpret it as a ceiling.

And they move on.

2 The Mediocre People Settle In

Mediocre performers watch leadership closely. If there are no consequences, they adjust their output accordingly. They won't sabotage you. They won't dominate either. They give you exactly what the environment requires.

No accountability = minimum effort.

And over time, the standard slowly drifts downward. Mediocrity becomes normal.

3 The Underperformers Multiply

Underperformers are not confused. They understand very clearly when there are no consequences. Weak leadership creates psychological safety for poor performance.

Deadlines slip.
Excuses increase.
Ownership disappears.

And because there is no correction, the behavior spreads. Culture is not defined by what you preach. It is defined by what you tolerate.

The Cultural Cost of Weak Leadership

When accountability disappears:

- Standards erode

- Resentment builds
- Performance declines
- Turnover increases
- Revenue eventually follows

And here is the brutal reality:

A culture without accountability always becomes a culture of frustration.

The strong grow frustrated. The average grow comfortable. The weak grow protected.

That is not sustainable at any phase of scale .

Accountability Is Leadership

Holding people accountable is not harsh.

It is clarity.

It is consistency.

It is respect.

When you set expectations, measure performance, coach consistently, and enforce standards, something powerful happens:

- High performers lean in.
- Average performers rise.
- Underperformers either improve or exit.

All three outcomes strengthen the organization. If you want to scale beyond the early growth phases, you must become comfortable with accountability. Because growth does not tolerate softness in standards. And leadership without accountability is not leadership.

It's avoidance.

And avoidance compounds just like excellence does.

Getting Results Through Others

At some point, your job shifts from:

"Doing the work."

To:

"Getting results through others."

That requires:

- Clear expectations
- Defined KPIs
- Written SOPs
- Consistent coaching
- Consequences for underperformance

Accountability is not aggression. Delegation is not abdication. Leadership is not control.

It is clarity + courage + consistency.

Good. Now we're getting to the root of it.

Because accountability without culture becomes enforcement. And culture without clarity becomes chaos.

Culture: The Invisible Force Running Your Company

Here's the truth most owners ignore:

You already have a culture. Every company does.

The only question is whether you **designed it intentionally** or whether it formed accidentally.

If you did not clearly establish it, then it was shaped by:

- The strongest personality in the room
- The longest-tenured employee
- The loudest voice
- Or the path of least resistance

So, take a moment to reflect on those points, who are those people. Are those people who you want establishing your company culture? If yes, then great, you are where you need to be, however, if not, you have some work to do.

Accidental cultures rarely serve the organization.

They serve comfort. They serve convenience. They serve whoever pushes hardest.

That is not leadership.

That is drift.

Mission. Vision. Values. Alignment.

Culture must align with:

- **Mission** – Why you exist
- **Vision** – Where you are going
- **Values** – How you behave while getting there

If your culture does not reinforce those three elements, you will constantly feel friction inside the organization.

You'll see:

- Mixed priorities
- Conflicting behaviors
- Unspoken resentment
- Decision paralysis

Because culture answers the question:

"How do we behave here?"

If that answer is unclear, everyone invents their own.

Hire for Alignment, Not Just Skill

Too many leaders hire for experience and hope values work out later. That is backwards. You can train skill. You cannot train character. You can teach process. You cannot force alignment.

When someone's personal values conflict with company values, three things happen:

- Performance becomes inconsistent
- Trust erodes
- Cultural tension spreads

Look for people who align with your standards.

Look for:

- Ownership mentality
- Coachability
- Discipline
- Integrity
- Commitment to excellence

Not just resume bullets. When values align, accountability feels fair. When values misalign, accountability feels personal.

If You Don't Define Culture, It Defines You

Let me be Honest.

If you are frustrated with your team, look at your culture. If standards are low, look at what you've tolerated. If urgency is missing, examine what behavior has gone unchecked.

Culture is shaped daily by:

- What you reward
- What you ignore
- What you correct

- What you celebrate

And culture compounds. Just like revenue. Just like leadership. Just like mediocrity.

Final Leadership Standard

Strong culture + clear mission + enforced accountability = scalable organization.

Weak culture + unclear values + inconsistent leadership = turnover and stagnation.

As you move through the phases of scale , culture becomes increasingly critical.

At $100K, culture is personality-driven.
At $1M, culture must be principle-driven.
At $3M+, culture must be leadership-driven.

If you don't establish it intentionally, you will spend years trying to fix what formed accidentally. And that is far more expensive than building it correctly from the start.

The Leadership Edge

I've been leading people for 32 of my 35 working years.

- Military.

- Corporate.
- Entrepreneurial ventures.
- Coaching organizations.

Different industries. Same patterns. The organizations that scale are led by people who are relentlessly committed to improving themselves. Because leadership has a ceiling. And your company will hit it.

If you stop growing, so does your team. If your team stops growing, so does revenue. If revenue stalls long enough, regression begins.

Final Thought

If you are serious about building a scalable enterprise, ask yourself:

- Are you developing leaders beneath you?
- Are you upgrading your own leadership capacity?
- Are you hiring for attitude, ambition, and aptitude?
- Are you building a culture that top talent wants to stay in?

You don't build a multimillion-dollar business alone. You build it with a team. And that team will only go as far as you are capable of leading them.

That's not inspirational fluff. That's math.

Chapter 23

Customer Focus: The Profit Stabilizer

If you don't serve them well, someone else will.

After 24 years serving clients in retail, I can tell you this with certainty:

Your long-term success in business is directly tied to your ability to serve your clients exceptionally well.

Not adequately.
Not sufficiently.
Exceptionally.

Because if you don't meet their needs, they will go elsewhere. And they won't feel bad about it. Oh yeah, and they will tell everyone else as well, particularly in today's instant world of social media posts.

The Power of a 10 Out of 10 Experience

Before I was ever promoted into a regional leadership role in the wireless retail industry, I had already built the equivalent of a six-figure income.

Not because I had a better territory.
Not because I had better pricing.
Not because I had some secret product advantage.

I built it on client engagement. I built it on follow-up. I built it on service.

I developed a disciplined client follow-up system. Every customer interaction was tracked. Every promise was documented. Every opportunity to reconnect was scheduled.

But the real difference-maker was what happened at the end of every transaction.

I would look the client in the eye and say:

"Have I provided a level of service that would deserve a 10 out of 10 score?"

And then I would follow it with:

"Assuming I have, who else do you know that would benefit from the amazing experience I provided you today?"

That wasn't accidental. It was intentional.

Exceptional Service + Direct Ask = Revenue Growth

Here's what most business owners get wrong.

They think that if they provide great service, referrals will just happen.

They won't. We learned this the hard way. Most clients will not refer you simply because they had a good experience.

They need:

- A true 10 out of 10 interaction

- A reminder that they received it
- A direct invitation to share it

If you don't remind them, they move on with their day. Not because they didn't appreciate you. Because life gets busy. Referral generation is not passive. It is engineered.

Service Is a Strategic Lever

That simple two-question close did three things:

1. It forced me to hold myself accountable to delivering that 10 out of 10 excellence.
2. It created a moment of reflection for the client.
3. It opened the door for immediate referral opportunities.

And it worked.

Consistently.

That discipline, paired with structured follow-up, fueled income growth long before I stepped into regional leadership.

The Real Lesson

Exceptional service is not just about being kind or polite.

It is about:

- Creating an intentional experience
- Reinforcing the value delivered

- Converting satisfaction into advocacy

If you want market share, you must earn it. If you want referrals, you must ask for them. If you want loyalty, you must create memorable moments. And then you must remind your clients that you did.

That is not arrogance. That is professional discipline. Customer Experience is not just a feel-good concept. It is also a revenue strategy. And when executed intentionally, it compounds faster than almost any paid marketing channel ever will.

The Market Rewards Who Serves Best

Entire industries are built around one simple dynamic:

A consumer need is not being fulfilled well enough.

So, someone else steps in and offers:

- The same product
- The same service
- The same solution

But they do it:

- Faster
- More efficiently
- More conveniently
- More friendly
- More aligned with the client's values

And because of that, they capture disproportionate market share. Not because their product is dramatically different. Because their **experience is.**

Clients Vote With Their Wallets

Business owners often get frustrated when customers leave.

"We didn't do anything wrong."

Maybe not.

But you didn't do it:

- Fast enough
- Smooth enough
- Easy enough
- Personal enough

And the client makes the decision. Not you. People today have options. Endless options.

You are not competing against "bad businesses."

You are competing against:

- Better speed
- Better communication
- Better alignment
- Better experience

If you ignore that reality, the market will correct you.

Speed Has Become a Competitive Weapon

In the last 10 to 15 years, speed of service has become a defining factor in purchasing decisions.

Response time.
Delivery time.
Resolution time.

The company that answers first often wins. The company that resolves fastest earns loyalty. Delay creates doubt. Doubt creates alternatives. Alternatives create churn.

The Modern Client Is Evaluating More Than Price

Today's consumer evaluates more than just product and cost.

They consider:

- Eco-friendliness
- Faith-based alignment
- Social responsibility
- Brand values
- Cultural fit
- Transparency

You may not personally prioritize these. That's irrelevant. Your client does. Ignoring these evolving trends is not stubbornness.

It's strategic blindness.

Pay Attention to What Your Clients Pay Attention To

Customer experience is not a department. It is a discipline. It requires intentional systems.

You must:

- Solicit feedback consistently
- Make it easy for customers to provide input
- Actually listen
- Act on the data
- Communicate what changed

When a customer sees that their feedback resulted in a real improvement, loyalty increases exponentially. Silence kills trust. Responsiveness builds it.

Feedback Is a Growth Multiplier

Feedback loops must be built into your organization.

Not casually.

Systematically.

Use:

- Surveys
- Direct outreach
- Online review platforms
- Net Promoter Score tracking
- Post-service follow-up processes

But here's the key:

Don't just collect feedback. Respond to it publicly when appropriate.

Tell your customers:

- "You told us this."
- "We heard you."
- "Here's what we changed."

That level of transparency builds brand equity that marketing dollars alone cannot buy.

Customer Experience and Scale

As you move through the phases of scale, customer experience becomes more complex.

At $100K, you can manage it personally.
At $1M, you need systems.
At $3M+, you need departments and metrics.

If you fail to systematize customer experience, scale will magnify your weaknesses. Volume amplifies friction. Without structure, growth creates chaos.

Reputation: Built in Years. Destroyed in Hours.

You've heard the age-old adage:

It takes years to build a reputation and only hours to destroy it.

In today's world, it might not even take hours. It can take one poorly handled interaction.

One lazy employee.

One dismissive response.

One ignored complaint.

And suddenly:

- A one-star review lives online forever.
- A negative post spreads across social media.
- A frustrated client tells ten others.

Reputation compounds slowly. Damage spreads quickly.

Lazy Execution Is Not a Small Problem

Most businesses don't lose reputation because of catastrophic failure.

They lose it because of:

- Indifference
- Poor training
- Lack of accountability
- Unclear service standards
- Employees who don't understand the stakes

A lazy employee does not just cost you one transaction.

They cost you:

- Trust
- Referrals
- Brand equity
- Future revenue

And if leadership tolerates it, it becomes cultural.

Remember:

Culture is defined by what you tolerate.

If you tolerate mediocre service, you are choosing brand erosion.

Every Employee Is a Brand Representative

Every person on your team represents your brand.

Not just the sales team.
Not just customer service.

Everyone.

From the first phone call to the final invoice. You may have spent 10 years building credibility in your market. One careless interaction can undo momentum you spent a decade creating. And the market does not care how long you've been in business.

It cares how it was treated today.

Customer Experience Is a Leadership Responsibility

If your team mishandles customers, that is not a customer service problem.

It is a leadership problem.

It means:

- Expectations were not clear
- Standards were not enforced
- Training was not sufficient
- Accountability was missing

Exceptional customer experience does not happen accidentally.

It is designed. It is trained. It is reinforced. It is measured.

Protect the Asset

Your reputation is an asset. At higher levels of scale, it directly impacts enterprise value.

Buyers evaluate:

- Reviews
- Retention rates
- Brand perception
- Client loyalty

Poorly managed customer experience doesn't just hurt revenue.

It lowers valuation. It reduces multiples. It limits exit opportunities.

Final Standard

If you want to build a scalable, transferable business:

- Train your people relentlessly.
- Establish non-negotiable service standards.
- Hold employees accountable for how clients are treated.
- Address service failures immediately.

Because you can spend years building a trusted name in your market…

And one careless moment can light it on fire. Guard your reputation like its cash.

Because at scale, it is.

Customer Experience is not about being "nice."

It is about being:

- Intentional
- Responsive
- Aligned
- Efficient
- Consistent

Serve your clients exceptionally well, and they:

- Return
- Refer
- Advocate

Ignore the experience, and they:

- Leave
- Post reviews
- Quietly erode your brand

The market does not reward effort. It rewards value. And value is defined by the customer. Master this competency, and you don't just build revenue. You build loyalty.

And loyalty compounds far longer than any marketing campaign ever will.

Chapter 24

The 7th Core Competency

Innovation & Technology: Resilience in Change

Resilience in Change. Relevance Through Innovation.

Let's get something straight.

Technology has **always** shaped business. The printing press, the assembly line, the internet, smartphones. Every wave compressed time, eliminated middlemen, and punished the unprepared.

But what we're living through right now?

This isn't incremental. It's exponential.

Artificial Intelligence, specifically Large Language Models like ChatGPT, Claude, or Gemini have been publicly accessible for barely three years… and it's already rewriting job descriptions, collapsing service models, and redefining what "competitive advantage" even means.

Entire industries that once had 20 to 30-year lifecycles are now facing 3 to 7-year compression windows.

If that doesn't get your attention as a CEO, nothing will.

From "Built to Last" to "Built to Adapt"

I acknowledged earlier in chapter 16, having read *Built to Last* by Jim Collins, one of the benchmarks for being visionary was sustaining for thirty years or more. Longevity. Durability. Institutional excellence.

Thirty years.

Today?
Thirty years without meaningful reinvention is a liability.

Innovation used to be a department.
Now it is survival.

Innovation is not invention for invention's sake. It is:

The disciplined process of identifying what must change in order to remain relevant.

And now, with AI, the speed of required change has accelerated dramatically.

You don't get decades to ignore it.
You might get a few quarters.

Why Innovation Is Now a Core Competency

When I developed the original Six Core Competencies, they addressed the systemic reasons businesses fail:

- Leadership gaps
- Financial blindness
- Sales inconsistency

- Operational chaos
- People misalignment
- Weak client fulfillment

Those failures are well documented in the research . But as I continued working with over 140 clients, something became clear:

Even businesses that were operationally sound were being disrupted by technological acceleration.

Not because they were poorly run. Because they were slow to adapt. That's a different failure mode. And it demanded a seventh competency.

What Innovation & Technology Actually Means for a CEO

This is not about "being techy." This is not about posting AI quotes on LinkedIn.

This is about:

1️⃣ **Strategic Awareness**

Understanding how emerging technology affects:

- Your pricing model
- Your margins
- Your staffing structure
- Your customer expectations
- Your competitive landscape

If AI can reduce labor in your industry by 30%, and your competitor adopts it before you do, guess what happens to your margins? Theirs expand. Yours compress.

That's math. Not opinion.

2 Operational Leverage

AI and automation are force multipliers.

In the Micro and Start-Up phases , I already recommend leveraging AI tools for:

- Content creation
- CRM automation
- Client communication
- Admin workflows

At $100K in revenue, AI is leverage.
At $1M+, it becomes infrastructure.

By the time you reach Optimizer or Executive Phase, if you are not integrating:

- Automation into workflows
- Predictive analytics into forecasting
- CRM intelligence into sales processes
- AI into customer support

You are building a 1998 company in a 2026 world.

And the market will treat you accordingly.

3 Business Model Reinvention

Here's where most leaders freeze. AI doesn't just improve efficiency. It questions the necessity of entire roles and services.

If you:

- Sell information
- Provide analysis
- Offer advisory services
- Deliver repeatable content

You are already being disrupted. The right response is not panic. It's repositioning.

You must ask:

- What part of my value can be automated?
- What part must become more human?
- Where does trust, judgment, and leadership become more valuable as automation increases?

Because ironically…

The more AI advances, the more premium human leadership becomes.

The CEO Decision: Ignore, Experiment, or Lead

There are only three types of leaders right now:

1. **The Denier** – "This won't impact my industry."
2. **The Dabbler** – Plays with tools but never integrates them.
3. **The Architect** – Systematically builds innovation into the company's DNA.

Only one of those scales.

At My Biz Coaches, we are building innovation into our framework intentionally. We use AI to:

- Enhance client diagnostics
- Improve marketing efficiency
- Speed operational design
- Deliver insights faster

Not to replace leadership.

To amplify it.

The Compression Effect

Here's what most people don't understand. AI doesn't just improve companies. It compresses competitive distance.

A small, disciplined company leveraging AI can now compete with mid-sized firms. A $500K business using automation intelligently can operate with the efficiency of a $2M company. That changes the scaling equation.

It also means:

If you are complacent at $1M or $3M, a leaner, smarter competitor can leapfrog you. The moat is no longer size. The moat is adaptability.

Resilience in Change. Relevance Through Innovation.

That phrase matters. Resilience means you don't collapse when the market shifts. Relevance means you don't become obsolete when technology advances.

And here's the uncomfortable truth:

Most businesses won't fail because of poor effort. They will fail because they refused to evolve.

The Entrepreneur's New Reality

You are no longer just:

- A visionary
- A salesperson
- An operator

You are now:

A technology strategist whether you like it or not.

The businesses that will thrive over the next decade will not be the largest. They will be the fastest learners.

Why This Matters to Our Mission

Our mission at My Biz Coaches is clear:

Help 1,000 businesses achieve $1M+ in annual revenue without sacrificing their lives.

But in today's environment, that milestone requires:

- Leadership discipline
- Financial intelligence
- Sales mastery
- Operational excellence
- People development
- Client fulfillment
- And now… technological adaptability

Seven competencies.

Miss one, and growth stalls.
Miss innovation, and growth reverses.

Final Thought to Section II

In *Built to Last*, greatness was measured in longevity. In the AI era, greatness will be measured in adaptability. The question is not whether AI will impact your industry. It already has.

The real question is:

Will you integrate it intentionally…or will you react to it desperately?

Your competitors are deciding right now.

Section III

The 8 Phases of Scale

Chapter 25

The 8 Phases of Scale: From Creator to Investor

From Creator to Investor – The Evolution of a Real CEO

Let me be very clear.

Most business owners don't fail because they lack drive. They fail because they try to solve million-dollar problems with $100K thinking. Or worse, they try to operate a $10M business like it's still a side hustle.

Scale has phases.
Each phase demands a new version of you as the leader, founder, or CEO.

I've lived this personally; through 15 businesses, assisting in scaling companies past $100M, navigating acquisitions, and working with 140+ clients over the last six years. The pattern is clear:

What got you here will not get you there.

The 8 Phases of Scale provide clarity on:

- Revenue benchmarks
- Strategic focus
- Common traps
- Required leadership evolution

And no, revenue alone doesn't define success nor does it entirely determine the phase of scale, but it is a really accurate benchmark in most cases. Revenue does expose complexity. And complexity exposes leadership gaps.

Let's break this down.

Phase 1: Creator (Approximately 45% of all businesses are at this level)

$1 – $100K (Micro Business / Side Hustle)

You're vision-driven. Hands-on. Scrappy. This is survival through hustle.

Your Primary Focus:

- Get paying clients
- Validate proof of concept
- Deliver value
- Repeat

Opportunities:

- Speed and flexibility
- Low overhead
- Direct customer connection

Challenges:

- Inconsistent revenue
- Wearing every hat
- Emotional volatility

Critical Shifts:

- Move from idea to repeatable sales
- Track income and expenses immediately
- Stop pretending this is a hobby

Most businesses start here, and as referenced by the number of businesses (45%) that are still in this range, many stay there. As outlined in your early-stage breakdown, the emphasis is simple: Find clients, serve them well, and build momentum.

You are the bottleneck. And that's okay, for now.

Phase 2: Hustler (Approximately 25% of all businesses live in this realm)

$100K – $250K (True Startup)

Revenue-first survival mode. You're no longer "trying something." You're building something.

Primary Focus:

- Repeatable sales process
- First team members or freelancers

- Basic financial reporting

Opportunities:

- Early brand formation
- Process documentation
- Delegation begins

Challenges:

- Time management collapse
- Cash flow swings
- Delegation anxiety

This is where 25% of businesses fail in the first year and many more collapse shortly after.

Why? Because hustle without systems doesn't scale. This is where you must stop operating emotionally and start operating strategically.

Phase 3: Operator (At this threshold only about 15% of all businesses get to this level)

$250K – $500K

You're managing work and people now. This is where the consequences get bigger.

Primary Focus:

- Hiring intentionally
- Formalizing KPIs
- Documenting processes

Opportunities:

- Livable income
- Operational leverage
- Building culture

Challenges:

- Margin compression
- Overpaying yourself too early
- Poor documentation

This is where discipline wins.

You must:

- Monitor financials weekly
- Stay lean
- Develop middle management instincts

You are transitioning from doer to manager.

Most people resist that shift. That's why they plateau.

Phase 4: Leader (The last stop before the coveted $1 million, and only about 9% reach here)

$500K – $1M

Team-based, not task-based. This is the last big push before joining the top 10% of all businesses.

Primary Focus:

- Delegation improvement moving towards Mastery
- Sales process documentation
- Strong cash flow management

Opportunities:

- Department leaders emerging
- Brand visibility
- Real scalability

Challenges:

- Rising competition
- Marketing inefficiencies
- Founder control issues

Less than 10% of U.S. businesses ever hit $1M.

This is where you must:

- Work **on** the business
- Consider fractional executives
- Decide where your time creates highest ROI

You can't be everywhere anymore. Actually, you never could, but you tried and often got away with it, however, that won't happen nearly as often anymore. Learning to effectively get results through others is the most important skill to have developed and improved by the time you have reached this level. If you haven't, this is one of the primary skills that will keep you from reaching $1 million.

Phase 5: Architect (The coveted $1 Million threshold, about 6% reach this level, 4% stay here)

$1M – $3M

Designing scalable systems. Welcome to rare air.

Primary Focus:

- Profit optimization (15–20% target)
- Middle management strength
- Infrastructure investment

Opportunities:

- Enterprise value formation
- Acquisition exploration
- Strong brand positioning

Challenges:

- Complacency
- Weak long-term vision
- Incomplete leadership bench

Many businesses stall here because they're "comfortable."

Comfort kills scale.

This is where:

- Financial dashboards matter
- Strategic planning intensifies
- Vision must expand beyond income to enterprise value

Phase 6: Optimizer (At this level you are in rare air here, with only 1.5% of all businesses getting here)

$3M – $10M

Driving efficiency and margin. You are now building real wealth. Strategy and making time to strategically evaluate your business and all of it's components is the best use of your time, along with developing next level leaders.

Primary Focus:

- EBITDA growth
- KPI dashboards (7–10 core metrics)
- Leadership layering

Opportunities:

- 4x–6x EBITDA multiples to determine business valuation
- Strategic acquisitions
- Real estate and asset leverage

Challenges:

- Executive bloat
- Cultural drift
- Integration complexity

You are now managing leaders who manage managers. This phase demands emotional maturity and financial sophistication.

No ego. Just execution.

Phase 7: Executive (At this level, this is extremely rare air with only 0.4% reaching this level)

$10M – $25M

Leading leaders.

Less than 1% of businesses reach this stage.

Primary Focus:

- Capital allocation
- Strategic expansion
- C-Suite development

Opportunities:

- $3M–$5M+ annual profits, begin considering how to extract value from your business
- Board governance
- Institutional credibility

Challenges:

- Overexpansion
- Strategic misalignment

- Talent retention at executive level

You are no longer building a business. You are building an institution.

Financial strategy replaces cash flow management. Leadership development replaces personal production.

Phase 8: Investor (We're talking about the top 10% of the top 1% that reaches this level, or 0.1%)

$25M – $100M+

Capital allocation, M&A, and exits. You are now in the top fraction of a percentage. This requires real enterprise strategy. Decisions have significant consequences here. Getting access to the best Consultants and Advisors is likely well worth the investment. Everyone needs to be in the right seats to make this happen and the team needs to be solid. As the CEO, you're primary focus is key and identifying opportunities for growth, expansion, and beginning to built the exit ramp are all imperative now.

Primary Focus:

- Mergers & acquisitions
- Partial or full exit strategy
- Enterprise value maximization

Opportunities:

- 5x–10x EBITDA multiples
- Private equity interest
- ESOP or IPO potential

Challenges:

- Governance complexity
- Investor relations
- Succession planning

You must decide:

- Continue scaling?
- Install a CEO?
- Sell partially?
- Exit completely?

The options multiply, but only if the foundation is strong.

Chapter 26

Integrating the 7 Core Competencies into the 8 Phases of Scale

You Don't Arrive at Scale…You Graduate to It

And every graduation requires a different level of discipline across the 7 Core Competencies framework Most business owners don't stall because they lack hustle. They stall because they keep trying to solve a Phase 4 problem with Phase 1 skills.

Let's walk through the 8 Phases of Scale and get brutally clear about:

- What matters most at each level
- Where the competency gaps show up
- What must change to graduate
- And where I've personally seen this play out in real companies

The Phases of Scale Through the Lens of the 7 Core Competencies

(What matters most, where it shows up, and what graduates you to the next level.)

The 7 Core Competencies (The Non-Negotiables)

1. **Leadership & Vision**

2. **Financial Acumen**
3. **Sales & Marketing**
4. **Operational Excellence**
5. **People Management (Human Capital)**
6. **Customer Focus (Client Fulfillment)**
7. **Innovation & Technology** (*Resilience in change. Relevance through innovation.*)

This isn't a "pick your favorite three" framework. Most entrepreneurs naturally bring **1–3** of these. Scale requires you to solve for **all 7**, either by **hiring, partnering, or outsourcing** until you can build the function in-house.

Phase 1: Creator Phase - Micro Biz / Side Hustle ($0–$100K)

What matters most here

- **Sales & Marketing**: get customers, get paid
- **Customer Focus**: Deliver a great experience fast
- **Leadership & Vision**: Clarity before complexity
- **Financial Acumen**: Track money, don't guess
- **Innovation & Tech**: Use tools to move faster than your budget

Where it shows up

- Inconsistent revenue and inconsistent activity

- Overbuilding the "brand" before proving demand
- Doing everything manually and calling it "grinding"

What graduates you

- A repeatable way to get leads → close → fulfill → ask for referral
- Basic bookkeeping discipline
- Testimonials and proof

Personal example: In wireless, I learned early that profit is oxygen, it keeps you alive long enough for the next gasp of air. The stores that won at this phase weren't usually the prettiest. They were the ones that executed the same sales actions daily and followed up like their business relied on it, because it did.

Phase 2: Hustler Phase - Start-Up ($100K–$250K)

What matters most here

- **Operational Excellence**: Repeatable delivery
- **Financial Acumen**: KPIs start now, not later
- **People Management**: First hires, VAs, freelancers – The key is finding people to help
- **Sales & Marketing**: Expand channels without losing focus on the core
- **Innovation & Tech**: Automations, CRM, scheduling, invoicing

Where it shows up

- Owner becomes the bottleneck
- You "have clients" but lack consistency and capacity
- You start hiring… and realize hiring doesn't fix leadership problems

What graduates you

- Documented processes (SOPs) for onboarding + fulfillment
- A real CRM and follow-up system, that you and your team actually use
- Clear roles, expectations, and accountability

Personal example: My Biz Coaches didn't scale because of motivation. It scaled because we turned delivery into a system, not a heroic act. That shift is what unlocks the next phase.

Phase 3: Operator Phase ($250K–$500K)

What matters most here

- **Financial Acumen**: Cash flow discipline, pricing, margin control, strategic credit solutions
- **People Management**: Hire slowly, fire quickly (protect culture)
- **Operational Excellence**: CANI (constant improvement), measurable execution
- **Sales & Marketing**: Consistency becomes a competitive advantage

- **Innovation & Tech**: Scale your output without scaling payroll

Where it shows up

- Revenue rises but cash stays tight
- You start feeling the consequences of "winging it"
- Team drama appears if you haven't built leadership habits

What graduates you

- Weekly financial review cadence (non-negotiable)
- Margin-protected pricing model
- Team performance standards and training rhythm

Personal example: I've personally lived the lesson that revenue growth doesn't equal financial safety. If pricing is wrong or expenses are sloppy, growth just scales the problems faster.

Phase 4: Leader Phase I ($500K–$1M)

What matters most here

- **Leadership & Vision**: Shift from doer → leader
- **Sales & Marketing**: Document, train, and scale the sales engine
- **Operational Excellence**: Duplication is the game now
- **People Management**: Department ownership begins, start developing that next layer of leadership

- **Financial Acumen**: Stay engaged, don't "hand it off"
- **Innovation & Tech**: Tech becomes an investment, not a luxury
- **Customer Focus**: Raeputation drives referrals and deal velocit

Where it shows up

- Founder tries to brute-force to $1M
- You can't grow because you can't duplicate yourself
- Competition becomes visible through rising ad costs and price pressure

What graduates you

- Clear ownership by function (even if it's "player-coach" ownership)
- Operational documentation that supports training
- Stronger marketing experimentation, measured by ROI

Personal example: In scaling regions and helping push companies beyond $100M, the consistent pattern was this: Leaders stopped being the hero and started building the system that produced heroes.

Phase 5: Architect Phase ($1M–$3M)

What matters most here

- **Leadership & Vision**: Complacency is the silent killer; too many treat this as the destination
- **Financial Acumen**: Optimize expenses and deploy capital strategically
- **Operational Excellence**: Efficiencies and integration matter
- **People Management**: Leadership development and retention strategies are key
- **Customer Focus**: Build loyalty systems (NPS, retention, upsell)
- **Innovation & Tech**: Your edge becomes speed and automation
- **Sales & Marketing**: Brand + systems + expansion; new markets, regions, products

Where it shows up

- Plateauing at $1M because it "feels good enough"
- Owner dependency blocks transferability (and exit value)
- Weak middle management creates operational drag, or you can't keep good people

What graduates you

- Leadership bench: Managers who can run departments
- KPI dashboard discipline

- Strong client retention + upsell strategy (not just acquisition), primary scaling skill

Personal example: This is where "what got you here won't get you there" becomes painfully real. This phase rewards strategic leadership, not raw effort.

Phase 6: Optimizer Phase ($3M–$10M)

What matters most here

- **Leadership & Vision**: Become CEO, not head operator
- **Financial Acumen**: Enterprise value thinking (EBITDA, multiples, ROI)
- **Operational Excellence**: Feedback loops and measurable improvement
- **People Management**: Leaders managing leaders
- **Sales & Marketing**: Consistent engine with department heads
- **Customer Focus**: Retention + CX must scale
- **Innovation & Tech**: Infrastructure upgrades become mandatory

Where it shows up

- "We're successful" but still messy internally
- Ops drag increases unless you're disciplined
- Talent retention becomes a business strategy, not an HR task

What graduates you

- Strategic leadership team (COO/CFO-level capability)
- Clean financials and documented operations
- Measurable customer experience programs

Personal example: This is where I watched enterprise value become real during acquisitions. Once EBITDA is meaningful, every decision either increases value or steals it.

Phase 7: Executive Phase ($10M–$25M)

What matters most here

- **Leadership & Vision**: Governance, succession, strategic direction & alignment particularly in the middle-management areas
- **Financial Acumen**: Capital structure, ERP, forecasting maturity, reinvestment, tax strategies, etc.
- **Sales & Marketing**: Segmentation, predictive metrics, brand authority
- **Operational Excellence**: Automation and scale-ready systems
- **People Management**: Succession planning and executive development
- **Customer Focus**: Scalable CX systems (tech + training)
- **Innovation & Tech**: AI + automation + analytics as competitive moat

Where it shows up

- Board-level decisions start appearing (whether formal or informal)
- Execution depends on culture + leadership depth
- The business must run without the owner to be truly valuable, test your leadership teams

What graduates you

- C-suite strength and succession readiness
- Mature KPIs tied to forecasting and strategy
- Scalable customer systems and analytics

Personal example: This is the level where an exit becomes real, not theoretical. Buyers don't buy hustle. They buy transferable infrastructure, leadership depth, and predictable performance.

Phase 8: Investor Phase ($25M–$100M)

What matters most here

- **Leadership & Vision**: Enterprise-level strategy and market expansion
- **Financial Acumen**: Capital deployment, acquisition strategy, PE readiness
- **Sales & Marketing**: Market dominance initiatives
- **Operational Excellence**: Enterprise tech and supply chain automation

- **People Management**: Executive systems + incentive structures
- **Customer Focus**: Personalization at scale
- **Innovation & Tech**: AI-driven optimization and competitive insulation

Where it shows up

- Strategy becomes the job, not operations
- M&A becomes a lever, not a fantasy
- Tech maturity separates leaders from laggards

What graduates you

- Acquisition integration capability
- Elite leadership bench
- Scalable governance and operational excellence

The Real Graduation Rule (The One Nobody Likes)

You graduate from one phase to the next when:

- Results are repeatable
- Delivery is consistent
- Leadership is scalable
- Financials are visible and predictable
- Customer experience does not degrade with growth
- Innovation keeps you relevant
- The business becomes transferable

That's the Entrepreneur's Dream. And it's exactly why My Biz Coaches exists: To help business owners stop guessing, start executing, and build something that actually scales and ultimately sells.

Why We Cap the Model at $100M+

Simple.

Beyond $100M, complexity becomes industry-specific, capital-market-driven, and institutional. Additionally, with only the top 10% of the top 1% reaching over $25 million annually, statistically speaking most businesses will never reach this level. And, admittedly, this is as far as my experience and competence would carry this book. At least for now.

At this level:

- Public markets may influence direction
- Global expansion changes governance
- Strategy becomes macroeconomic

The purpose of this book is to guide entrepreneurs from startup to serious enterprise value.

The skills required beyond $100M are often less entrepreneurial and more corporate-capital-market-focused.

And most importantly…

Our mission at My Biz Coaches is to help 1,000 businesses reach beyond $1M or more profitably and build transferable assets.

That impact happens inside the $1M to $100M range.

The Real Lesson of the 8 Phases

Each phase requires:

- A new identity
- A new discipline
- A new skillset
- A new tolerance for complexity

Most businesses fail not because the market rejected them, but because the owner never evolved.

The failure data we studied shows recurring causes:

- Cash flow mismanagement
- Weak leadership
- Poor planning
- Inability to adapt

The 8 Phases of Scale give structure to prevent those outcomes. Scale is not random. It is sequential. And if you understand where you are in the model, you stop guessing. Additionally, should you find yourself on a rapid trajectory of growth, you'll be able to pay attention to the challenges that are arising and identify them as a normal course of growth, rather than another distressing challenge that needs to be overcome.

You start executing.

That's how you move from Creator… to Investor.

And that's how you build something that lasts.

Section IV

Exit, Transferability & Legacy

Chapter 27

From Startup to Exit: Begin with the End in Mind

Why 80% of Businesses Never Sell… and What the 20% Do Differently

Let's start with the uncomfortable truth. Most business owners think they're building an asset. Most are actually building a job with overhead. In reality, most are building **a job with overhead**.

The business depends on them for sales.
For decisions.
For client relationships.
For operational problem-solving.
For nearly everything that makes the business function.

Remove the owner, and the machine stops.

From the outside, it may look like a business. From a buyer's perspective, it looks like a **risk.** And buyers do not purchase risk. They purchase **predictability**.

You've heard the statistics. I've heard it from brokers, M&A advisors, accountants, attorneys, valuation experts, and financial planners across hundreds of conversations with professionals who live inside the transaction world.

Nearly **80% of businesses that go to market never sell.**

Not "sell for less."

Not "take longer to sell."

They simply…**do not sell.**

That's not just a statistic.

That's a serious wake-up call for very current business owner!

Because behind every one of those failed sales is a business owner who believed they were building something of lasting value.

- Someone who worked late nights.
- Sacrificed weekends.
- Took risks.
- Signed personal guarantees.
- Carried the stress of payroll and uncertainty for years.

And when the moment finally arrives to convert that lifetime of effort into financial freedom…

The market says:

"There's nothing here we can or want to buy."

The Moment Most Owners Never See Coming

Imagine this scenario. You've spent 20 or 30 years building your company.

You've built a good reputation.
You've made a decent living.
Your family has benefited from the income the business produced.

But now you're tired. Or maybe you're ready for the next chapter. So, you decide it's time to sell.

You contact a broker. They review your financials. They look at your systems. They evaluate your leadership team. They analyze the company's ability to operate **without you.** And after weeks of due diligence, they give you the answer most owners never expect.

The business may be profitable…but it isn't **transferable. Meaning no one will be willing to buy it.**

No systems.
No leadership team.
No documented processes.
No predictable revenue engine that runs independent of the founder.

In short:

The buyer would simply be **buying your job.** And most buyers already have one.

The Harsh Reality

A business only becomes valuable when it can survive **without the person who built it.**

Buyers look for three things:

1. **Predictable revenue**
2. **Repeatable systems**
3. **Leadership that can run the business without the founder**

If those three ingredients are missing, the business becomes incredibly difficult to sell. Not impossible. But unattractive. And in a market where buyers potentially have thousands of options, unattractive businesses sit on the shelf until eventually…they quietly disappear from the market.

Why This Happens to So Many Owners

The reason is simple. Most entrepreneurs never start their business with the **end in mind.** They start with a skill. A trade. An idea. Or a passion.

They become excellent operators. But no one ever taught them how to build a **transferable enterprise.** So, the business grows around them instead of beyond them. The owner becomes the center of the business ecosystem.

The decision maker. The rainmaker. The problem solver.

Which feels powerful while the business is growing. But it becomes a liability when it's time to exit.

The Difference Between the 80% and the 20%

The businesses that successfully sell do something fundamentally different. They build with **transferability** in mind. From early on, they begin designing the company as a **system**, not a personality.

They document processes. They build leadership teams. They create predictable marketing and sales engines. They track performance metrics that make the business understandable to outsiders.

In other words:

They build a company that a stranger could run. Because the moment that becomes possible, the business transforms from **a job** into **an asset.**

And assets are what buyers pay for.

This Is a Legacy Conversation

For many entrepreneurs, the business represents far more than money.

It represents decades of:

Effort.
Sacrifice.
Identity.
Family security.

For some, it is the vehicle that funded college educations, homes, and retirement savings. For others, it is the thing they hoped would create generational wealth.

But if the business cannot be sold…

Then the wealth never converts. The owner simply works until they decide to stop. And when they stop, the business often fades with them. That isn't a business legacy. That's a career.

The Question Every Owner Should Ask

At some point, every business owner must ask a difficult question:

If I stepped away from my business for 12 months…

Would it continue to grow? Or would it slowly unravel?

That question reveals the difference between **ownership** and **employment inside your own company.**

And it's the question that determines whether your business becomes part of the **80% that never sell**…

or the **20% that create real enterprise value.**

This Is Why the 7 Core Competencies Matter

Over decades of building, acquiring, scaling, and exiting businesses, one pattern became painfully clear. The companies that succeed long term are not lucky. They are disciplined.

They consistently develop the **core competencies** required to build a durable organization.

Leadership.
Financial clarity.
Sales and marketing systems.
Operational discipline.
Human capital development.
Customer focus.

And today, more than ever…

Innovation and technological relevance.

Because the modern business environment is evolving faster than ever before. Industries that once lasted decades now change in years. Businesses that fail to adapt likely will become obsolete before they ever reach their exit opportunity.

The Real Opportunity

Here's the encouraging part. This outcome is **not predetermined.** A business can transition from owner-dependent to enterprise-ready.

It requires intention.
Structure.
Leadership growth.

And a clear understanding of **what makes a business valuable in the first place.** That is exactly what this book is about.

build **transferable companies** will not just build income. They will build **assets.**

Assets that create freedom.

Assets that create wealth.

Assets that become a legacy.

Human beings have a strange habit of waiting until the end of the journey to ask the question that should have been asked at the beginning.

"Am I building something that will last?"

For business owners, that question may be the most important one you will ever answer.

The 6 Primary Reasons Businesses Don't Sell

(Insights reinforced through my preparation for a podcast with Walt Lipsky, a 38-year business broker and former President of the Arizona Business Brokers Association and echoed by nearly every one of the hundreds of professionals I have engaged with in the exit ecosystem.)

After interviewing brokers and studying upwards of a thousand transactions, the same six issues surface repeatedly:

1 The Business Is Too Dependent on the Owner

If you are the rainmaker, the operator, the relationship holder, the decision hub, and the brand…

You don't own a business. You own employment with liability. Buyers purchase **cash flow that survives the owner.** If revenue collapses when you leave, valuation collapses with it. This is why transferability is everything.

If revenue depends on you personally:

- Your relationships
- Your technical skill
- Your charisma
- Your daily involvement

Then the buyer isn't acquiring a company. They're acquiring risk.

Every serious buyer asks one question early:

"What happens if you disappear for 90 days?"

If the answer is "everything stalls," the valuation drops instantly. This could equate to a 50%, even a 75% reduction in valuation, depending on how many factors of the business are directly impacted by the exiting owner.

Transferability drives value. Dependency destroys it.

2 Financials Are Messy or Unclear

Buyers don't buy hope. They buy verified numbers.

When financials are inconsistent, commingled with personal expenses, or lack clean reporting, buyers discount aggressively or walk away.

The irony?

Many owners discover their real margins for the first time when a broker asks for clean EBITDA.

If you can't articulate:

- EBITDA (Earning Before Interest, Taxes, Depreciation, & Amortization)
- SDE (Seller's Discretionary Earnings)
- Cash flow consistency
- Customer concentration risk
- Recurring revenue percentage

You're not ready to sell. And that's fine. But pretending you are? That's expensive. No clean books. Personal expenses mixed in. No reliable monthly reporting. No defensible EBITDA.

Sophisticated buyers don't guess, they won't even engage in the conversation.

They might discount.

If they can't see:

- Consistent revenue trends
- Clear margin structure
- Documented cash flow – I mean well documented and confirmed
- Customer concentration ratios

They assume the worst. And sophisticated buyers always price in risk.

Now, there are other players that might show up to consider buying your business. They consist of the Confused Buyer, the Cautious Buyer, and the Unsophisticated Buyer.

Confused buyers don't decide, they sit on the fence for a long time unsure if they are sitting on a goldmine or a landmine. They could drag out a sale discussion for a year or longer and never pull the trigger.

Then there is the Cautious buyer, they will just run. Fully convinced they are about to get sold the magic pill that they know doesn't exist.

Unfortunately for the seller, what is left is the unsophisticated buyer who doesn't know what they don't know. Then, they use money they really should not use to buy a business that is nothing more than what has now become a highly leveraged liability of a job. And, if they can't keep up the payments, the buyer likely will get the business back in shambles and will be left trying to rebuild or close it down.

3 Unrealistic Valuation Expectations

This one is emotional.

Owner's price based on:

- Years of sacrifice
- Emotional attachment
- "What I need to retire"

- Gross revenue instead of profitability
- Ego

Markets price based on:

- EBITDA
- Risk profile
- Industry multiples
- Sustainability

If your business generates $400K in SDE (Seller's Discretionary Earnings) and the market multiple is 2.5x, the number is not $3M because you feel it should be. It's $1M and that assumes everything else matches up.

It doesn't matter that you've worked 70 hours a week for 12 years.

Buyers are not buying your grind. They are buying future earnings. The market is not sentimental.

And overpricing is the fastest way to kill momentum in a deal.

Lack of Strategic Preparation

The most common cause of failed exits?

The owner waited too long to prepare.

Quite honestly, you should have been identifying what your exit strategy was from the day you decided to start the business and likely have a few different options to be able to effectively pivot to if necessary. This improves your odds of exiting on your own terms. Because let's face it, you are going to exit your business one day, however, will it be on your terms or someone else's?

Businesses under $3M in revenue (as a reminder, this represents about 98% of all businesses in the US), typically exit for one of four primary reasons:

- Divorce
- Health issues
- Family obligations (parents health, spouse relocation, etc.)
- Burnout

That means the exit is reactive. Reactive sellers negotiate poorly. Strategic sellers create bidding environments.

Preparation should start 3–5 years before you ever list.

Almost no one does. According to a recent study, in the unusual circumstances that someone decided to proactively prepare for a sale, they often assume that 12 months is a sufficient amount of time. This is often not even close to enough time, particularly depending on the size and amount of effort spent on preparing to sell.

At My Biz Coaches, we provide a program that will usually take between 18 and 36 months to adequately prepare a business for exit, and that is with an established strategic plan, highly selected personnel, and years of experience.

5 Undocumented SOPs (Standard Operating Procedures)

If the way your business runs lives inside your head… you don't have systems.

You have memory. And memory is not transferable.

Buyers want:

- Documented onboarding processes
- Fulfillment workflows
- Quality control systems
- Vendor management procedures
- Escalation protocols
- Financial reporting cadence

If processes are undocumented, the buyer assumes:

- Transition will be chaotic
- Performance will dip
- Key employees may leave
- Customers may churn

Undocumented SOPs increase perceived risk. And perceived risk reduces multiples. You cannot scale what you cannot duplicate. And you cannot sell what you cannot duplicate.

This is why Operational Excellence is not optional.

6 Undocumented or Unproven Duplicatable Sales & Marketing Strategies

This one quietly destroys enterprise value.

If your sales growth is driven by:

- Your personal relationships
- A single referral source
- Word of mouth
- One large client
- An undocumented "we just hustle" strategy

Then growth is not predictable. And predictable growth is what buyers pay premiums for.

Buyers want to see:

- Documented sales process
- Defined lead sources
- Conversion metrics
- Customer acquisition cost (CAC)
- Lifetime value (LTV)
- Channel performance tracking
- Repeatable marketing campaigns

If revenue cannot be systematically reproduced, the buyer assumes:

- Growth may stall
- Lead flow may dry up
- Customer churn may spike

Unproven marketing = unstable future earnings. Unstable earnings = lower valuation.

If you cannot show that revenue generation is engineered, not accidental, you will not command premium multiples. Sales & Marketing must be duplicatable, or it's not an asset.

What This Really Means

When you step back, these six reasons all point to the same underlying issue:

Most owners build income streams. Few build transferable enterprises.

A transferable enterprise has:

- Independent leadership
- Clean financials
- Market-aligned valuation
- Long-term preparation
- Documented systems
- Engineered revenue generation

That is not accidental. It is designed. You spent years building revenue. The question is whether you're building value. Revenue feeds you today. Transferability creates real value which feeds you at exit.

And if your goal is legacy, liquidity, or leverage, you had better start building for the buyer long before you ever need one.

Why Most Children Don't Want the Business

Here's another uncomfortable truth. Your children saw the stress. They saw the long nights, the financial pressure, the arguments, the missed vacations.

You call it legacy. They sometimes call it sacrifice.

Unless you've intentionally developed:

- Leadership bench strength
- Clean systems
- Predictable income
- Cultural alignment

Your children may not want to inherit chaos. And forcing generational transition without preparation often destroys both the business and the family dynamic. Legacy requires design.

The Math of Longevity (It's Not in Your Favor)

From we know:

- Nearly 50% fail within five years
- Roughly 70% fail within ten

Now stack this with the 80% non-sale rate.

The probability of:

1. Surviving 10+ years
2. Becoming transferable

3. Selling successfully

Is dramatically smaller than most entrepreneurs want to believe. Statistically speaking, if you do what most owners do…

You will get what most owners get. Which is not an exit windfall. It's a slow fade-out. If you want a different outcome, you must operate differently.

How Many Owners Seek Financial Advice Before Selling?

When speaking with M&A advisors and financial planners, the pattern is clear:

Owners above $3M in revenue are significantly more likely to:

- Engage financial planners 3–5 years before exit
- Work with CPAs to optimize tax structures
- Clean up financial reporting
- Reclassify expenses
- Reduce discretionary noise

Owners below $3 million? Most call a broker first. That's backwards. Tax strategy before sale can mean hundreds of thousands of dollars, sometimes millions missed out on.

Structuring Smarter Exits

If you want to reduce taxes and increase liquidity, consider strategic structuring:

Partial Sale

Pull equity off the table while retaining upside.

De-risk personally. Continue scaling.

Seller Financing

Increase deal viability. Expand buyer pool. Potentially earn interest income.

ESOP (Employee Stock Ownership Plan)

Transition ownership internally. Tax advantages can be possible.

Asset vs. Stock Sale

Structure matters. The tax implications are drastically different.

Installment Sale

Spread tax burden over years.

Holding Company Structure

Separate real estate from operations.

Recapitalization with Private Equity

Sell majority stake, retain minority for "second bite of the apple."

There are more tools than most owners realize. But they require planning, often years in advance.

Why Owners Regret Selling

Another theme repeated across dozens of broker and advisor conversations:

Many owners regret selling.

Weeks later.
Months later.
Years later.

Why?

Because their identity was fused to the business. For 15, 20, 30 years, the company wasn't something they owned. It was who they were. When that disappears, so does structure, purpose, and daily relevance. Money does not replace meaning. If you do not design life after exit, the exit will feel like a loss; not a win.

The Deeper Issue: Identity Attachment

We associate our value with our businesses far too often.

Revenue becomes validation.
Title becomes identity.
Growth becomes ego.

When we detach ownership from identity, exits become strategic.
When we attach identity to ownership, exits become emotional.
And emotional sellers make poor negotiators.

The Echo Chamber of Professionals

Across:

- Business Brokers
- Accounting firms
- M&A advisors
- Estate planners
- Merchant services reps
- Payroll companies
- HR consultants
- Attorneys

The same conversations repeat:

- "I thought it would be worth more."
- "I didn't realize I needed three years of clean books."
- "My son doesn't want it."
- "I'm exhausted."
- "I wish I had prepared earlier."

Patterns are predictable. Which means outcomes are preventable.

Transferability Is the Real Asset

If your business:

- Operates without you
- Has documented SOPs
- Has diversified customer base

- Has clean financials
- Has leadership bench strength
- Produces consistent EBITDA

It becomes attractive. Attractive businesses create leverage. Leverage creates options. Options create legacy.

What You Must Do Differently

If you want to be in the minority that both survives and sells:

1. Master all Core Competencies, not just the ones you're good at.
2. Build systems that operate independent of you.
3. Clean your financials years before exit, or all along ideally.
4. Reduce customer concentration risk.
5. Develop leadership depth.
6. Consult tax and M&A professionals early.
7. Separate your identity from your enterprise.

You do not "prepare to sell" when you want to sell. You build to sell from day one.

Legacy Is Intentional

Legacy is not:

- A building
- A logo
- A website

- A valuation multiple

Legacy is:

- The leaders you developed
- The culture you built
- The wealth you structured wisely
- The impact that survives you

If you build correctly, you can:

- Scale
- Hold
- Sell
- Partially exit
- Step back
- Or continue growing

If you don't build correctly, the market decides for you. And markets are not sentimental.

You have two choices. Build a business that consumes you. Or build one that eventually frees you. Only one of those creates real legacy. Choose wisely.

Section V

Summing It All UP

Chapter 28

The Entrepreneur's Dream: Discipline, Scale, and the Path Forward

Doing it Alone, or Getting Some Real Help

Ok, let's bring this home. You've just walked through why businesses fail, how they stall, where they plateau, and what it actually takes to scale from **$0 to $100M+** without becoming another statistic.

You've seen the data.
You've seen the patterns.
You've seen the framework of The 7 Core Competencies aligned against the 8 Phases of Scale.

Now the only question that matters is this:

Are you going to try to muscle through it alone… or build the right support system around you?

The Truth Most Founders Don't Want to Hear

You are likely the bottleneck. There, I said it, it's out there, now we all need to own it. The reality is this is true for all of us. Worse yet, we lack the objective perspective to see what we can't see.

Not because we're incapable.
Not because we lack drive.
Not because we don't care.

But because no founder naturally brings strength in all seven competencies:

- Leadership & Vision
- Financial Acumen
- Sales & Marketing
- Operational Excellence
- Human Capital Management
- Customer Focus
- Innovation & Technology

Most entrepreneurs bring **1-3 naturally**. The market requires mastery of all seven.

That gap?
That's where businesses stall.
That's where exits fail.
That's where 80% of listed companies never sell.

And that is exactly where companies like **My Biz Coaches step in.**

From Startup to Exit — We Walk the Entire Journey with you

My Biz Coaches was not built as a traditional coaching or consulting firm.

It was built because I saw a systemic problem:

Business owners were hiring fragmented solutions.

- A marketing consultant here.
- A bookkeeper there.
- A sales trainer for a quarter.
- An operations "fix" when things broke.

It's reactive. It's incomplete. It's expensive. And it rarely builds a transferable asset. We've built something different.

A Complete Scaling Infrastructure with a guide and a map.

We serve business owners across every phase:

Phase	Revenue	Primary Need
Creator	$0–$100K	Proof of concept, sales tractions
Hustler	$100K–$250K	Systems & repeatability
Operator	$250K–$500K	Lean scaling & KPIs
Leader	$500K–$1M	Leadership development & delegation
Architect	$1M–$3M	Profit optimization & infrastructure
Optimizer	$3M-$10M	Enterprise value creation
Executive	$10M-$25M	Leading Leaders
Investor	$25M - $100M	Capital Allocation, M&A, Exits

And at every level, we assist in solving the competencies required at that stage.

Not hypothetically. Strategically. Practically. Systematically.

What We Actually Do for Clients

Let's remove the fluff.

Here's how we help:

1 We Diagnose Clearly

Through competency assessments and phase identification, we pinpoint:

- Where you are.
- What's missing.
- What's breaking.
- What's limiting enterprise value.

No guessing. No ego. Just data.

2 We Tell You the Truth

If you're the bottleneck, we say it. If your margins are weak, we show you. If your leadership is misaligned, we address it. Most founders don't fail from ignorance. They fail from avoidance. We won't let you allow that.

3 We Provide the Right Solution at the Right Phase

There are only three ways to solve competency gaps:

1. Hire for it
2. Partner for it
3. Outsource it

In early stages, we provide fractional and outsourced solutions.

As you grow, we help you:

- Build SOPs
- Create job descriptions
- Install KPIs
- Recruit intentionally
- Structure leadership properly

Because the goal is not dependency. The goal is independence with infrastructure.

We Bring the Ecosystem

We offer access to:

- Fractional CFOs
- Fractional CMOs
- COOs
- Sales leaders
- HR consultants
- Marketing agencies
- M&A advisors
- Banking partners
- Capital connections

Hundreds of aligned professionals tied to the Core Competencies. You don't need to figure out who to trust. We've already vetted them and provided you with a list of options to choose from.

Client Success Stories

You want proof. Good. Here are a few of our favorites.

From $0K to $400K in 24 Months. Partnerships can be hard so make sure you have a solid agreement. No plan is perfect, so being flexible is key. And personal growth is always necessary for business growth.

This client was referred to me by a common associate. This client was not my ideal client and as such I almost chose not to engage. However, their passion for their business, their belief, and the recognition that their service was in high need led to what has evolved over the last few years.

- Initially, we assisted the client in documenting a business plan, conducting budget forecasting, and identifying next steps.
- Helped the partners outline and document an operating and partner agreement.
    - Recommended law firm to assist and document this process.
- Assisted client to identify, select, and negotiate first site location.
- Introduced client to bookkeeper, accountant, payroll provider, HR services, merchant services, marketing solutions, and banking services.

- Assisted owners in getting access to over $250K in business credit and lines of credit.

Result:

- Owners went from concept to executed business and earning profits in less than 1 year.
- In just two short years, clients are already highly recognized in their local community and in their spere of influence as a significant contributor in their space. Additionally, they have established a high level of credibility for their services in their industry.
- Business is poised to move into their next generation location which will be twice their previous size to support the growth, and will increase revenues by between 50% to 100% in coming year.

From losing $10K per month to profiting $25K per month in 18 months. Sometimes, it's not just what you know, it's also who you know. If at first the plans are not working, look at what is and pivot accordingly.

When we engaged with this client, they were about $100K in debt and losing about $10K per month after about 8 months in business. Within the first 6 months and along with some challenging decisions and important changes, the business reached break-even, made some key new hires, and pivoted their business model. Just over 1 year later the business had completely pivoted into a new area of practice, greatly improved productivity, and grown the business to $300K. By year 3 the business had improved enough to move to an ideal facility and increased revenues to over $550K and on pace this year for $1 Million.

- Encouraged strategic decision to remove under-performing key employee, allowed for new key employees which launched company to 2.5X revenues.
- Helped identify key service solution providers, guided marketing focus to revamp website and improve SEO, assisted in guiding through payroll and HR services selection, including a strategic partnership which bridged the gap during key transition.
- Tightened financial tracking, introduced implementation of strategic debt reduction strategies, assisted client to go from denied loan for $15K, to over $250K in credit and lines of credit, in just over 6 months. Assisted in moving a HELOC with a personal guarantee on home to a new loan to the business, with no personal guarantee.
- Assisted owner through second key employee transition and likely a third, which will allow organization to move to $1 Million annually this year.

Result:

- Scaling to $1 Million within 3 years, operating a profitable business without burning out employees, and finding the ideal area of business required discipline, patience, and creativity which we were able to help provide during this process.

- Despite my client being an excellent operator, when you don't know what you don't know, you make mistakes that are costly. By providing insights to my client that they were not aware of previously, this allowed them to pivot accordingly and unlocked significant growth opportunities.

- With $1 Million on the horizon for this client, that is just the beginning of their potential. They are adding at least 1 to 2 new key employees allowing this client to potentially reach $3 Million to $5 Million annually in the next few years. Providing meaningful employment to her team, a rewarding business for herself, and very productive business that could be sold when the owner is ready.

After 22 years in business, finding new levels of success and productivity. When you have run the same operation for that long, you often lose perspective of what could be better in your business, and you just might need a bit of "Objective Perspective".

Image a company operating for 22 years very successfully and then having a breakout year where revenues grow by 50% and profits double, year-over-year. Yes, that is real, and we were the catalysts for the change.

What caused the break-thru?

Jolting leadership complacency, cleaning up undocumented operations, and a general unwillingness to innovate. Technology can have significant impacts, and even very simple solutions can provide insight and understanding of your business, allowing you as the owner to focus on the more impactful portions of your business.

Solution:

- Restructured leadership roles
- Built SOP library
- Introduced strategic planning cadence

Within 24 months:

- Revenue doubled
- EBITDA improved significantly
- Enterprise value multiplied

Why Our Model Works

Because it's comprehensive.

We don't just improve marketing strategies; we also review the sales process and adjust accordingly.

We don't just fix finances, we identify cashflow challenges, improve business credit solutions, improve reporting strategies, introduce better partners for improved visibility and better options.

We assist you to align:

- Vision
- Numbers
- Systems

- People
- Clients
- Innovation
- Exit strategy

Simultaneously.

Fragmented coaching produces fragmented results.

Integrated coaching builds scalable assets.

Our Billion Dollar Mission

Our mission is bold:

Help 1,000 businesses profitably reach $1M in revenue.

Why?

Because only about 6% do.

And because reaching $1M, if done properly, changes everything:

- Higher survival rates
- Stronger margins
- Improved Exit potential
- Stronger Wealth creation
- True Freedom – Both operationally as well as financial when done correctly.

And from there, scaling to $3M, $10M, or beyond becomes realistic.

For Founders Reading This

You do not need to struggle alone. You do not need to guess your way through growth. You do not need to and should not "hope" you'll figure out an exit strategy later.

Hope is not a scale strategy. Structure is.

For Coaches, Consultants, and Fractional Executives

If you are a professional who serves business owners:

You know this truth. No single coach solves all seven competencies. That's why we are building something larger than individual practices. A collaborative, competency-aligned model.

A movement of professionals who understand:

Business growth is multidisciplinary. If you want to serve clients at a higher level, with deeper impact, inside a proven framework, aligned with a billion-dollar mission…

There is room at this table.

The Most Comprehensive Business Coaching Model for Small Business Owners

We are not the cheapest. We are not transactional. We are not motivational fluff.

We are:

- Data-driven.
- Phase-specific.
- Competency-aligned.
- Exit-aware.
- Systems-focused.
- Results-obsessed.

From $1 to $100M. From side hustle to enterprise. From survival to scalable assets.

Final Thought

The small business failure epidemic is real. But it is not random ,it's predictable.

And because it is predictable…

It is solvable!

You now have the framework. The only remaining variable is whether you execute alone…

Or build with the right guide beside you using the map we help you create. We are here for the journey.

From Startup to Exit.

And every messy, uncomfortable, transformational phase in between.

To Your Success!

BONUS:

The 7 Core Competencies & 8 Phases of Scale Assessment

Powered by My Biz Coaches

The My Biz Navigator™ assessment and the associated app were created to solve a very specific problem:

Business owners don't need more noise. They need a diagnostic.

The foundation of the app is built on two integrated frameworks:

- The **7 Core Competencies of a Successful Business Owner**
- The **8 Phases of Business Scale**

Individually, these models are powerful.
Integrated together, they become transformational.

Why the Assessment Exists

Most owners overestimate their strengths and underestimate their blind spots.

They think:

- "Sales is my issue."
- "Marketing is broken."
- "I just need more capital."
- "If I could just hire the right person…"

But in reality?

They're operating with 2–3 competencies developed…
in a phase that demands 5–7.

That misalignment is expensive.

The My Biz Navigator™ assessment and app were built to:

1. **Objectively evaluate competency strength**
2. **Identify phase-of-scale positioning**
3. **Expose bottlenecks**
4. **Prioritize next best actions**
5. **Deliver a structured growth roadmap**

No guessing.
No motivational fluff.
Just clarity.

What the My Biz Navigator™ App Actually Measures

The platform evaluates business performance across the 7 Core Competencies:

- Leadership & Vision
- Financial Acumen
- Sales & Marketing
- Operational Excellence
- Human Capital Management
- Customer Focus
- Innovation & Technology

These are not theoretical categories.

They were forged from decades of experience watching what separates the 6% who reach $1M from the 94% who don't.

The app also identifies which of the 8 Phases of Scale you're operating in; from Creator / Micro Biz to Investor Phase

Because what works at $250K will break you at $1.5M.
And what works at $3M will collapse at $12M.

Context matters.

How It Works

The Assessment produces:

1 A Competency Scorecard

You see where you are strong.
You see where you are weak.
You see where you are dangerously average.

2 Phase Alignment Analysis

Are you operating like a Hustler when you need to be an Architect?
Are you leading like a Creator when you should be functioning as a CEO?

This mismatch is often the silent killer.

3 Risk Indicators

The app flags patterns that correlate with:

- Cash flow collapses
- Culture breakdown
- Sales stagnation
- Owner burnout
- Exit failure

Remember: nearly 80% of businesses listed for sale never sell. That's not bad luck. That's structural weakness.

4️⃣ Priority Action Map

Instead of 47 things to fix, you get:

- The top 3 focus areas
- The phase-specific corrections
- The competency gaps to close first
- A recommendation of next steps to act on

Execution > inspiration.

Why This Changes the Game

Most coaching is reactive.

We built something diagnostic and predictive.

Instead of:
"I feel stuck."

We get:

"Your Operational Excellence is lagging behind your Sales growth at Architect Level. That imbalance will create margin compression within 6 to 12 months."

That's leadership clarity. And clarity compounds.

Designed for Owners. Built for Scale.

The App supports:

- Startup founders trying to break $100K
- Growth-phase operators pushing toward $1M
- Mature companies optimizing EBITDA
- Owners preparing for acquisition
- Coaches and Fractional Executives who need structured insight for clients

It creates a shared language between:

- Founder
- COO
- CFO
- Sales Leader
- Marketing Team
- Advisory Board

No more debating symptoms.
We diagnose systems.

The Real Objective

This tool supports our broader mission:

Empower 1,000+ businesses to reach $1M+ in revenue, profitably, without sacrificing their life to do it.

That milestone is not arbitrary. Only about 6% of businesses ever achieve it.

And the difference between those who do and those who don't is rarely intelligence.

It's structure.
It's discipline.
It's alignment.

The Assessment and App provide owners a mirror. Sometimes that mirror is uncomfortable.

But growth requires honesty.

Final Thought

You cannot scale what you cannot measure.
You cannot fix what you cannot see.
And you cannot exit what is not transferable.

The 7 Core Competencies and 8 Phases of Scale were designed to provide clarity.

The Assessment and App were built to operationalize that clarity.

And once you see the gaps clearly…

You can finally build with intention instead of hope.

Click Here to view the My Biz Navigator™

References / Sources

Section 1 – Why Businesses Fail

[1] [9] [14] [15] Percentage of Businesses That Fail | LendingTree

https://www.lendingtree.com/business/small/failure-rate/

[2] [13] What Percentage of Businesses Fail? [2025]

https://clarifycapital.com/blog/what-percentage-of-businesses-fail

[3] [24] [39] [41] The #1 Reason Small Businesses Fail - And How to Avoid It | SCORE

https://www.score.org/resource/blog-post/1-reason-small-businesses-fail-and-how-avoid-it

[4] [10] [11] [16] [17] [20] [22] [23] [25] [26] [27] [29] [33] [40] [44] [45] [46] [47] [50] Top Reasons Small Businesses Fail (How to Avoid Them) | CO- by US Chamber of Commerce

https://www.uschamber.com/co/start/strategy/why-small-businesses-fail

[5] [34] [35] [38] [49] 6 Reasons New Businesses Fail

https://www.investopedia.com/financial-edge/1010/top-6-reasons-new-businesses-fail.aspx

[6] [8] [18] [19] [32] [36] The Top 10 Reasons Businesses Fail & How To Avoid It

https://fibrecu.com/reasons-businesses-fail/

[7] [12] [37] [42] [51] Small Businesses Fail for Consistent Reasons | University of Georgia Small Business Development Center

https://georgiasbdc.org/small-businesses-fail-for-consistent-reasons/

[21] [28] [30] [31] [43] [48] What percentage of businesses fail and why?

https://capsulecrm.com/blog/what-percentage-of-businesses-fail/

About the Author

Eric T. Whitmoyer does not write about business from theory. He writes from repetition, pressure, failure, recovery, and scale.

Over the course of more than 30 years, Eric has built, led, acquired, scaled, and exited businesses across multiple industries. He owned or acquired 15 companies of his own, including ventures scaled past $1 million and a trucking company grown to more than $6 million annually. Many of those businesses were built while he simultaneously served in senior executive leadership roles. This was not accidental. It was the result of disciplined systems, effective delegation, and a structured approach to the core competencies that drive sustainable growth.

As a key executive in the wireless retail industry, Eric helped lead two companies past $100 million in annual revenue through strategic expansion, acquisitions, operational discipline, and leadership development. In 2017, the company he assisted in building successfully exited, ending his final corporate role, after contributing to its significant growth and enterprise value creation. That exit solidified a hard truth: businesses that scale properly create options. Businesses that do not create dependency.

Those experiences shaped the foundation of this book.

Eric's career has never been built on hype, shortcuts, or motivational slogans. It has been built on measurable results. Over $1.3 billion in sales have flowed through organizations he has led or influenced. He has managed complex operations, overseen multi-state expansion, navigated acquisitions, built executive teams, and corrected broken systems under pressure. He has seen what works; and more importantly, what fails.

After his corporate exit, Eric founded My Biz Coaches with a clear mission: to help 1,000 business owners achieve the Entrepreneur's Dream; building a profitable, scalable company that surpasses $1 million in annual revenue without sacrificing their health, family, or sanity in the process. Fewer than 6% of businesses ever reach that milestone. Eric believes that statistic is not a law of nature; it is a competency gap.

Through My Biz Coaches, Eric and his growing team of coaches, consultants, and fractional executives guide business owners from startup to exit. They focus on closing gaps across the seven Core Competencies outlined in this book: Leadership, Financial Acumen, Sales & Marketing, Operational Excellence, Human Capital Management, Customer Focus, and Innovation & Technology. Rather than offering fragmented advice, Eric built an integrated model designed to help owners build transferable enterprise value.

In addition to his coaching work, Eric hosts The Biz Coach Show, where he shares practical, data-driven insights on growth strategy, mergers and acquisitions, leadership development, operational efficiency, and marketing performance. His content is direct, structured, and actionable; because business owners do not need more noise. They need clarity.

Eric's background also includes service as a decorated military veteran and experience as a former competitive champion kickboxer; disciplines that reinforced resilience, accountability, and the importance of preparation under pressure. Those principles now shape how he approaches business transformation: disciplined execution over emotional decision-making.

This book represents the synthesis of decades of pattern recognition, observing why businesses fail, identifying where founders become bottlenecks, and developing a repeatable framework that increases the probability of sustainable success.

Eric does not claim business is easy. He believes it is earned.

And for those willing to approach it with structure, discipline, and the humility to solve their competency gaps, he believes scale is not only possible; it is predictable.

Work With My Biz Coaches

Option 1: The 7 Core Competency Assessment (Starting Point)

If you're serious about growth, we begin with clarity - Because guessing is expensive.

We evaluate:

- Revenue stage alignment
- Profit margins & financial controls
- Sales process maturity
- Operational documentation
- Leadership structure
- Team performance & retention
- Client fulfillment & retention systems

You receive:

- A competency scorecard
- Phase-of-scale alignment
- A 90-day strategic action plan
- Clear Hire vs Partner vs Outsource recommendations

Schedule Your Strategy Call
https://bit.ly/AssessmentMeeting

Option 2: Fractional & Advisory Support

For founders between $250K and $5M who need execution support, not inspiration.

We provide:

- Fractional CFO / CMO / COO support
- Sales process design & training
- KPI dashboards & financial modeling
- SOP documentation & operational redesign
- Leadership development & succession planning
- AI and Automation implementation solutions

You don't need an executive salary, you need executive-level thinking applied strategically.

Learn More About My Biz Coaches Fractional Executive
https://mybizcoaches.com/fractional-executives

Option 3: Scale to $1M Accelerator

Less than 6% of businesses ever reach $1M in revenue. That's not a coincidence.

We built a system specifically for:

- $100K–$750K founders
- Stuck operators
- Burned-out hustlers
- Owners who are the bottleneck

This program integrates:

- Revenue acceleration
- Profit optimization (15–20% target margins)
- Delegation & leadership shift
- Process documentation
- Exit-readiness mindset from Day 1

Because building something you can't sell isn't scale. It's self-employment with stress.

👉 *Apply for the $1M Pathway*
https://mybizcoaches.com/1m-accelerator

Option 4: Exit & Enterprise Strategy

For $3M–$25M businesses preparing for:

- Acquisition
- Partial liquidity
- Strategic merger
- Succession transition

We focus on:

- EBITDA expansion
- SOP institutionalization
- Transferable sales systems
- Leadership bench strength
- Enterprise value maximization

Because 80% of businesses listed for sale never sell.
And most owners don't find that out until it's too late.

☞ *Book an Exit Strategy Consultation*

https://mybizcoaches.com/advanced-exit

See Eric Speak

Eric T. Whitmoyer, Founder & CEO, My Biz Coaches
Author of *The CEO's Playbook for Scale* & Host of The Biz Coach Show

Eric Speaks on:

- The 7 Core Competencies & 8 Phases of Scale Frameworks
- Why 94% of businesses never reach $1M
- Why 80% of Businesses that List Never Sell
- Building enterprise value from Day One
- Hire vs Partner vs Outsource vs AI strategies

Interactive keynote includes the "Scale-Up Sprint" workshop experience

See Speaking Topics & Book Eric
https://bit.ly/EricWhtimoyerSpeaking

Join the Mission (For Coaches & Fractional Leaders)

If you are:

- A sales strategist
- A C-Suite Executive
- An operations implementation expert
- A leadership coach or people & culture consultant
- Any Professional that serves Business Owners

And you're tired of watching clients fail because they're only solving 1 area of business.

We are building a collaborative ecosystem of professionals who serve business owners.

Solo coaching caps impact. Integrated support multiplies it.

In our mission to help 1,000+ businesses reach $1M+, we offer:

- Tech stack solutions & proven marketing strategies
- Brand recognition & collaborative cohorts
- Lead generation support
- Cross-functional client engagements
- Revenue participation model, and so much more…

☞ *Apply to Join the Biz Mastery Network*
https://bit.ly/BizMasteryNetwork

Our Billion Dollar Mission

We are on a mission to help **1,000 business owners profitably reach $1,000,000 in annual revenue.**

That's not motivational fluff.
That's structural intervention in a broken entrepreneurial system.

If you are building…
Scaling…
Stuck…
Or preparing to exit…

You don't need another podcast episode.
You need alignment across the competencies that actually drive enterprise value.

From Startup to Exit — We're There for Your Biggest Decisions.

👉 Schedule the Call.
👉 Explore the Framework.
👉 Or Join the Team.

But don't stay in the 94%.

Made in the USA
Monee, IL
04 November 2026

67379640R00154